the FANTASTIC LIFE®
revisited

How to Get It, Live It and Pass It On®

R CRAIG COPPOLA

the FANTASTIC LIFE® revisited

Dedicated to Bill Lee (1942-2021)

You became the best of what a mentor and friend can be and for that I am eternally grateful. I think about you every day and miss you. God bless you, Bill.

the FANTASTIC LIFE® revisited

If you purchase this book without a cover you should be aware that this book may have been stolen property and reported as "unsold and destroyed" to the publisher. In such case neither the author nor the publisher has received any payment for this "stripped book."

This publication is designed to provide competent and reliable information regarding the subject matter covered. The author and publisher specifically disclaim any liability that is incurred from the use or application of the contents of this book.

©2023 by R. Craig Coppola.

All rights reserved. Except as permitted under the U.S. Copyright Act of 1976, no part of this publication may be reproduced, distributed, or transmitted in any form or by any means or stored in a database or retrieval system, without the prior written permission of the publisher.

Any registered trademarks referenced in this book are the property of their respective owners.

Published by

6040 E Montecito Ave
Scottsdale, AZ 85251

ISBN # 9798987179307

Library of Congress Control Number: 2022921859

Printed in the United States of America

Second Edition: 2023

03-24-23

Thank you to all the people in my life and in this book. You have made my life richer, more fulfilled, meaningful and…Fantastic.

Thank you to Kathy Heasley for your time, patience, discussions, and mad writing skills.

the FANTASTIC LIFE® revisited

- Dedication
- Introduction – The Fantastic Life Truths PAGE 1

1. **Know Your Stories** PAGE 18
2. **Be Crystal Clear on What You Want** PAGE 44
3. **Build Your Resumes Every Year** PAGE 62
4. **Play Where You Can Win** PAGE 82
5. **Get a Win** PAGE 102
6. **Set Goals** PAGE 120
7. **Stay Out of The Gap** PAGE 138
8. **Use the 2% Rule** PAGE 154
9. **Recognize There are Two Kinds of Pain** PAGE 174
10. **Take the Decision Out of the Moment** PAGE 194
11. **Don't Waste Time** PAGE 214
12. **Do Nothing in Moderation** PAGE 236

- Consistency PAGE 256
- About R. Craig Coppola PAGE 265

the **FANTASTIC** LIFE ® revisited

Welcome to day 1 of YOUR Fantastic Life.

Together we'll be walking through the 12 Rules that, over decades of living, coaching, and observing, I have found essential to becoming the person you want to be and having the life you want. As you read this book, know that it is experiential. Everything in it I live consistently every day of my life, so nothing is theoretical. I think about it. I practice it, experiment with it, and talk to people about it. Some of them you'll meet in this book. They are among the most successful people I have had the pleasure of knowing. They are friends, business associates, and, inspirations to me. They exemplify the 12 Rules in action, so I hope their fantastic stories inspire you as well.

Before we dive into the heart of The Fantastic Life / Revisited, know this is the second edition of this book. It is entirely new and filled with more real-world stories and depth that took me years to live and acquire—the years between the first edition and this one. A lot has happened in my own Fantastic Life, and it has made this book richer in its context.

I still love *The Fantastic Life* original book. It's written how I think. Short, concise, and to the point. It's filled with questions to ponder, so if you want more background and interaction, you can always read the original book before or after this one. They really are two different books.

The first version of this book had 18 Rules. This one has 12. The reason is that a few of the rules are now what I view as Truths, rather than directives to follow and more something to recognize as forces working in all our lives. What are these truths that will come into play as you begin and live your Fantastic Life? The following is my list.

Fantastic Life Truths

All Life is Connected As you work through this book and begin thinking in terms of goals and choices, you'll quickly find that The Fantastic Life is one of priorities and trade-offs. What you do in one area of your life will impact other areas. And the effort you put toward one important thing will impact the time and energy you have to dedicate toward something else. Clarity of choice is essential *(see Rule #2)*.

Live your values When you give your all, when you go for your Fantastic Life, you'll have no choice but to live your values. Otherwise, you just won't find the effort meaningful enough, the decisions you have to make reflexive enough, and the drive to actually live your Fantastic Life won't be forceful enough. The work will be hard, maybe not "worth it," and you won't get the adrenaline rushes along the way. Your values are your guide, so if you haven't had time to reflect on what those are, reading this book will likely be your time to do just that. Do you have to know your values right now, up front? No. They will present themselves as you progress. But as you read and work through this book, make a point of examining your values. Redefining them. Growing them.

5 | Introduction

Recognize you will grow The person you are right now will not be the person who comes out the other side of this book and the work within it. You'll be a person who is more focused and who accomplishes more than 99% of your peers. You may have people in your life who want to come along and have a Fantastic Life too. Great! Buy them the book. Do it together. But you may have people around you who don't want you to change and grow. These may be friends and family members. Don't let them limit you. You may have to limit your time with them and see it for what it is: That you are moving forward and they are not.

Believe there are no limits In this book, you'll hear me say several times that you can be and do anything. You just can't be and do everything. Choices are an important part of your Fantastic Life. Those things you choose to do can be limitless. And they won't be pie-in-the-sky dreams that never get accomplished. Because built into the Fantastic Life are the methods and the mindsets for achieving whatever goal you choose. One more thing, this is not a book to read in one sitting and put away. It's a book to be used, pulled out, thought about, dog-eared, bookmarked, annotated, tested, and ultimately put to work in your life. Nothing happens without action.

Introduction

I mentioned that in this version of the book, *The Fantastic Life / Revisited*, I have had some help from people I admire. These leaders have achieved so much, and they have done so by living by the Fantastic Life Rules. **Here's who you will meet in this book.**

BILL LEE (1942-2021) ▌ *Bill had an illustrious career in Commercial Real Estate that spanned nearly four decades. In 1979, he founded Lee & Associates, a commercial real estate company with a dynamic new business model. The company was, and continues to be, owned equally by its transaction shareholders, a concept that created a sense of shared responsibility and cooperation throughout the organization. Today, Lee & Associates is the fourth largest real estate sales organization in the country, with 54 offices, over 900 brokers and 450 equal owners. Bill oversaw much of this tremendous growth before retiring in 2008 to pursue his hobbies of surfing, gardening, owning a bed and breakfast, and spending time with family and friends. He is greatly missed by all who were fortunate enough to know him.*

READ MORE ABOUT BILL
Chapter 1 – Know Your Stories

CHARLIE DUNLAP Since 1972 Charlie has owned, constructed, and/or managed over 13 million square feet of real property assets valued at more than $2 billion. Later he provided real estate consulting to the financial industry on another $2.4 billion in loans and eventually became a direct real estate lender funding $1.25 billion in loans to date.

READ MORE ABOUT CHARLIE
Chapter 6 – Set Goals

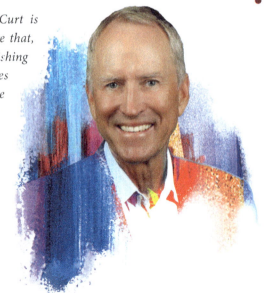

CURT G. JOHNSON Curt is a real estate investor, but before that, he was instrumental in establishing the National Commercial Services Division at First American Title Insurance Company, and served as President and Vice Chairman of the company. He was a CRE broker prior to his career with First American.

READ MORE ABOUT CURT
Chapter 8 – Use the 2% Rule

DANIELLE FEROLETO Danielle is the President and CEO of Small Giants, a full-service marketing agency in Scottsdale, Arizona. Danielle has dedicated the last 25 years of her career to growing companies in the commercial real estate and construction industry through marketing. She is recognized for her strategic approach, strong networking practices, creative marketing strategies, and practical training skills. Danielle is heavily involved in many industry organizations and was recently appointed to the Arizona State University (ASU) Alumni Board of Directors. She is an industry mentor and coaches the next generation of industry leaders through her work as an adjunct professor at ASU and at Small Giants.

READ MORE ABOUT DANIELLE
Chapter 5 – Get a Win

DEAN BLOXOM The capstone of Dean's 43-year-career was the founding of imortgage with his business partner Jay Johnson. Together, they built the company to 2,500 employees and several billion dollars a year in mortgage volume. Part of their success was maintaining a family atmosphere no matter how quickly they grew or how big the company became. Today he spends his time in several business ventures and with his growing family. According to Dean, "Grandkids make everything worth it!"

READ MORE ABOUT DEAN IN
Chapter 7 – Stay Out of the Gap

STEPHEN MCCONNELL Stephen has owned and operated Solano Ventures, an AZ-based Private Equity firm for the last 30 years. He holds ownership positions in over 50 companies and still manages to stay fit and focused on his health—which is a priority in his life. Another priority is his relationships. Stephen lives in Scottsdale today with Cathy, his wife of 38 years and has two grown children, Chris and Courtney.

READ MORE ABOUT STEPHEN
Chapter 11 – Don't Waste Time

MARIA LUNA *Maria is a serial entrepreneur, who sold her previous company and became the co-founder, and CEO of FAMIGO, a platform that lets content creators make money from their work. She holds an MBA from McCombs Business School and was in marketing for Fortune 500 companies including Abbvie, BMS, Mayo Clinic, and Nabisco. She also is well versed in international business development and speaks several languages fluently. When she is not creating high-value companies, Maria volunteers for minority entrepreneurship programs, animal rescue causes, and enjoys painting and writing.*

READ MORE ABOUT MARIA
Chapter 8 – Use the 2% Rule

FRED PAKIS *Fred co-founded JDA Software, Inc. (now Blue Yonder) in 1985 and served as President and Co-CEO for various periods of time through 2000. Blue Yonder is Arizona's largest software company with over 5,000 employees and revenues in excess of $1 billion. The company is headquartered in Scottsdale, Arizona, and operates in over 70 locations around the globe. Blue Yonder was acquired by Panasonic in September 2021 at a valuation of $8.5 billion.*

READ MORE ABOUT FRED
Chapter 10 – Take the Decision Out of the Moment

the FANTASTIC LIFE® *revisited*

MIKE LIPSEY *Mike is President of The Lipsey Company, and internationally recognized as the leader in training and consulting for the commercial real estate industry. His keen insight into the business of commercial real estate spans over forty-five years. Mike has developed over 200 courses tailored to the commercial real estate industry. As the industry's leading trainer, coach, and consultant, few people affect the day-to-day sale, lease and management of the commercial real estate industry as does Mike.*

READ MORE ABOUT MIKE
Chapter 12 – Do Nothing in Moderation

MIKE WELBORN *Mike has been blessed with a wonderful spouse, Patricia, and three great, (now adult) children. His career as CEO, president and chairman spans the mortgage, banking, restaurant, and healthcare industries. His track record in all those industries is one of high growth and winning cultures. Mike and Pat have served on numerous for-profit and community boards and have been on 21 bicycle trips around the world.*

READ MORE ABOUT MIKE
Chapter 4 – Play Where You Can Win

MICHELLE HEEB Michelle is the president & CEO of Forward Tilt, which since 2013 has been building beautiful, functional workspaces that put people first and capture the individual company's personality. That is Michelle's passion. Today, it is one of the premier women-owned certified dealerships in the nation and has achieved unsurpassed growth, while maintaining the highest standards. It's all about developing and executing strategies while enhancing culture and creativity. Michelle takes great pride in her work and the spaces she helps bring to life!

READ MORE ABOUT MICHELLE
Chapter 2 – Be Crystal Clear on What You Want

ROBERT KIYOSAKI Best known as the author of Rich Dad Poor Dad — the #1 personal finance book of all time — Robert Kiyosaki has challenged and changed the way tens of millions of people around the world think about money. He is an entrepreneur, educator, and investor who believes the world needs more entrepreneurs. With perspectives on money and investing that often contradict conventional wisdom, Robert has earned an international reputation for straight talk, irreverence, and courage and has become a passionate and outspoken advocate for financial education.

READ MORE ABOUT ROBERT
Chapter 1 – Know Your Stories

STEVE JOHNSTON Steve is a technology sector expert in finance, team building, and customer acquisition. Prior to entering the airline software space Steve founded Front Street Technologies Inc., a long-distance reseller that he later sold. He then founded Genetic Diagnostics Inc., a DNA testing company that he took public in Toronto. Steve doesn't shy away from doing the hard work and that's a key to his success. He holds a Mechanical Engineering degree from the Technical University of Nova Scotia and a Bachelor of Science in Mathematics & Physics from Mount Allison University.

READ MORE ABOUT STEVE
Chapter 9 – Recognize There are Two Kinds of Pain

SHARON HARPER As CEO, chairman and co-founder of Plaza Companies, one of Arizona's leading real estate firms, Sharon oversees all facets of company operations, including the ownership, development, leasing, and management of nearly 13 million square feet of commercial real estate. Sharon is also one of Arizona's most respected civic and business leaders with extensive involvement throughout the community.

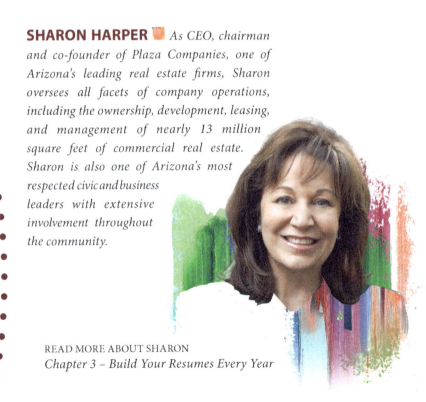

READ MORE ABOUT SHARON
Chapter 3 – Build Your Resumes Every Year

Now it's time for you to seize your Fantastic Life. Jump in and know that as you read this book, you'll be able to find more resources at TheFantasticLife.com. Congratulations, you're on your way to becoming one of us now. The accomplished few who are living and loving a Fantastic Life.

the FANTASTIC LIFE® revisited

Everyone
who is living,
including you,
has stories with
a beginning,
and a middle,
but no end.

Fantastic Life Rule
Know Your Stories

Everyone has a story. Actually, everyone has quite a few stories. These are the stories we tell ourselves every single day, throughout the day—365 days a year. Trust me, the stories never stop. Wait until you start seeing and recognizing the stories you tell yourself. "I'm too fat." "I'm too lazy." "I always lose." Or "I'm the greatest." "I can't be stopped."

You also have biographical stories. You've probably heard the classic one in the business world. "I went to such and such college and got a degree in (fill in the blank). When I graduated, I started my career at a big firm and, within a few years, realized it wasn't for me. So I took all the money I had saved, which wasn't much, and bootstrapped my own shop." What are your versions of that story?

From there, the stories continue to where our storyteller is at the present moment. It's the stories—so far. Your stories are "so far," too, and you are shaping and refining them with every breath you take. Whatever your stories, know that their nuances make them unique to you. You're the only one who has lived this life to this present moment and feels the way you do.

Everyone who is living, including you, has stories with a beginning, and a middle, but no end. Because they are in the middle of "so far." I see these stories as having two different parts. The first part is the one you're writing with every passing day. The second part is how you reframe the first. **If you truly want to live a Fantastic Life, your stories must continue to evolve—positively.** If your stories evolve negatively, if they devolve, it is because you may have other stories inside that you may or may not be aware of. They are the stories in our heads that keep us stuck. They're stories we tell ourselves about ourselves. These stories live within our thoughts and have been created throughout our lives by the world around us and our mental, emotional, and spiritual responses.

Let's just say right now that these other stories—and the tellers of these stories—can be a real barrier to you living your Fantastic Life. If your storytellers keep reminding you that, "You have no business trying to start your own company. Who do you think you are? You're not VP material. It's never going to work, you know. You're not smart enough. It's too risky; stick with what's safe. Go off to Paris alone? You don't even know the language. You'll get taken advantage of. You're a dreamer." and so on... If you listen to that non-sense, you'll never do anything to advance yourself, your abilities, your real story, and subsequently, live your Fantastic Life. The truth here is that your "other" stories and their storytellers are the ultimate limiters.

What Are Your Stories?

Your stories need not limit you. All your stories can be your ultimate champions! Isn't that great news? **When you dare to have Fantastic Life big rock goals, the key is to simply do the work to bring the stories in your head into alignment with the stories you want to live.** In other words, let's get the stories you hear in the silence of the night, in the morning when the alarm goes off, or on the weekend to be very close to the story you share when someone asks, "So tell me about you." Sound easy? It is, and it isn't.

Author James Clear says, "The events of your past are fixed. The meaning of your past is not. The influence of every experience in your life is determined by the meaning you assign to it. Assign a more useful meaning to your past, and it becomes easier to take a more useful action in the present." What he is saying is that you are in command. It might not feel that way yet, but it will.

This book, *The Fantastic Life / Revisited*, takes the earlier version of this title and expands it into new realms, providing more everyday context to the Rules I introduced years ago so that you can see the patterns more easily and apply them to your own life.

The life I am living is not the same as the life that wants to live in me.

You'll find familiarity and meaning that I hope will inspire you to both begin and to keep going. And in this chapter, we'll focus on learning to recognize the stories we are telling ourselves, modify them, and become the champion of our own life. This is the power of this rule. You are becoming the person you want to be. It starts now. It starts here, and it starts with John.

In the first book, I introduced readers to John, whom I met while running the Marathon des Sables. The race is a 150-mile self-supported ultra-marathon in the Sahara Desert. No lie, that's what it is, and enduring it is even harder than it sounds. Running takes incredible physical, mental, emotional, and spiritual strength to get through the long days and nights in the Sahara's triple-digit heat and towering sand dunes, with no end in sight.

John's story is an excellent example of a successful guy whose biggest accomplishment was overcoming his storyteller father's painful words that John endured when he was a child. "You're lazy. You'll never amount to anything," John's father used to say to his son over and over. John could have decided to align his own life experiences with his father's destructive words and beliefs, affirming them in his life. But instead, John decided—I mean literally made the decision—that his father's story wasn't the one he wanted for his life. He decided to create a new story, a more Fantastic story, and begin living it. At age 18, John left home and joined the Navy, where he excelled.

I met John while running the race, at an aid station on a 50-mile segment, as the sun was setting, feeling exhausted and irritated by the sand in our shoes and every other part of our bodies, having run about ten straight hours up to that point. I came to learn that he taught U.S. Navy enlistees how to swim. He told me that to train for this race, he would get up in the darkness and head to the pool before anyone else arrived and run for two hours around the pool. Then he'd do his job, run another hour at lunch, and finally run two more hours after work. He did all of this wearing full firefighter gear. Consistently, day in, day out. Month after month. "This guy must have some crazy story to cause him to train like this," I thought.

There was a lot of time to talk and a lot of time to think during the race, and I couldn't help but marvel at John, who decided not to believe the story his father told him. Who decided not to let that story be the story he would tell himself in the silence of the night. The story he decided to create was one he could prove to himself over and over again in ever more Fantastic ways. Right there is when I decided two things: First, I decided I would run with him because there was no way he wouldn't finish even if he had to crawl, so he'd be great mentally for me. And second, I decided from that moment on I'd be like John and let the stories I tell myself cultivate, curate, refine, and drive me to live my Fantastic Life. Guess what? It's working, for decades now. My life, my past, and my stories empower me to live a Fantastic Life.

You Can Choose Your Story

A Fantastic Life isn't one of just accomplishing incredible feats, however, one after the next. A Fantastic Life is about the journey itself and the empowering feelings that accompany achieving incredible feats. (Being as goal-oriented as I am, it took me a long time to be able to not only write this but actually mean it.) It's a life that often involves choosing and then doing the hard things which, when achieved, give you a sense of accomplishment, a sense of pride, and the peace of knowing you are living life in full color. These choices and actions happen all the time. Sometimes by the minute.

Being Fantastic requires real-life decisions and actions at every turn, which isn't always easy. Your stories have to be powerful enough, meaningful enough, and personal enough to move you inch by inch through your Fantastic Life. This path gives you an ever-increasing confidence and belief in your abilities. A Fantastic Life is executing, over and over again, and embedding your Fantastic stories—both the ones you tell yourself and the ones you tell others when asked—deep in your soul.

One of my long-time friends and business partners is Robert Kiyosaki. **Robert is the author of the #1 personal finance book of all time, Rich Dad Poor Dad, and many other books about gaining financial freedom. He's been at it for decades and has been credited with inspiring more people to entrepreneurship than anyone in human history.** In a way, Robert's "choice" of occupation was likely more about knowing the story in his head and applying it in a way that ultimately made himself and millions more successful in life.

Here's the abridged version of Robert's story. The first thing to know is that Robert's dad was a school teacher and later a superintendent of schools in Hilo, Hawaii. He was Robert's "Poor Dad." The dad of Robert's best friend developed hotels and motels in Honolulu and, you guessed it, was Robert's "Rich Dad." Robert's real dad was not poor in the literal sense. He was poor in how he viewed the world—how people who live average or below average lives view it. Specifically, they believe that you "go to school, get good grades, get a college degree, get a job, work hard and eventually retire. That's life," as Robert would often put it.

Robert's Rich Dad saw the world differently. He saw life as an investor who let money work hard for him. And not just his own money, but other people's money too. "My Poor Dad did everything he could never to have any debt. And my Rich Dad used debt to make himself a fortune." Robert, who loved the idea of money from an early age, followed his Rich Dad's example, not his Poor Dad's, and became a worldwide success.

That's the story, but another story, one that played out in Robert's head for years—and truly became a catalyst for his success—was much different. It's a story that could have

SETH GODIN SAYS: "Feeling like a failure has little correlation to actually failing."

just as easily made him a failure, a person who gives up on life or settles for what naysayers believed him to be. You see, Robert, the son of an educator, was a terrible student. He barely made it through high school. "Why sit in class when you can surf? So we'd skip school a lot." And teachers of the day were brutal, labeling him as stupid and as a person who would never amount to anything. Robert endured school, and teachers endured Robert. Imagine how hard that must have been, particularly when your dad works in your school.

Robert did manage to graduate high school, but the continual pounding by teachers and his dad took a toll on him. How could it not? Knowing he was expected to attend college, he applied and got accepted into the United States Merchant Marine Academy. "I chose a military academy because I knew I would need a disciplined environment to be successful. And this particular military academy over the others, because I found out its graduates earned more money than the graduates from any of other military academy." Robert's stories, including his love of all things money and his need to overcome his story of not being good enough, were beginning to align.

True to form, he got a high-paying job on a freighter after graduation. Later, he went on to lead the nation in sales for Xerox, at the time a premier business training ground that led to many entrepreneurial success stories, Robert's among them. All this proved to Robert that school, grades, and often the dismissiveness of his teachers, didn't mean a darn thing in life. And that his Poor Dad's "pathway to success" was a myth, which in 1996, when *Rich Dad Poor Dad* was first published, was near heresy. The book was bold, relatable, and transformative. It was the true alignment of Robert's two stories—his aspirations of success and his distaste for the myths surrounding it—blended with just enough ire to plow through the many hurdles of business and life. His inner story is his power. That is when I met Robert. His stories, his views, and how he lived his life were empowering to me too.

Your Stories Are Connected

Knowing your stories and curating your stories, along with the milestone moments within each of them, are far more important than most people think. They have led you from where you were to where you are. If you have not taken the time to really discern the stories in your life, now is the time. It is also time to develop the habit of continuous review and refinement of your internal stories. Some only arise in certain situations, like when you are with your parents, siblings or old friends, for instance. Others trigger because of something that happens in your day. Take the time to jot them down in the moment before the opportunity slips away. When you go back and read what you wrote, you'll be glad you did.

Here's one more real-life example of how your stories shape your life from my dear friend and business partner. **Bill Lee, who passed away in 2021, was the founder of Lee & Associates, the commercial real estate firm that I have worked at as one of the founding principals in the Arizona office since 1991.** His story was the catalyst for Lee & Associates. And it remains the inspiration for thousands of commercial real estate professionals using Commercial Real Estate to enable their Fantastic Life.

Like Robert, Bill struggled in school as a child. He had what we know today to be Attention Deficit Disorder (ADD), and that made sitting still and paying attention in the classroom next to impossible. "My mind would just wander, no matter how hard I tried. I would create my own mental journeys and make my own decisions on those journeys. In a way, it trained me for my future because through that, I became daring as a teenager and young adult." Bill said he wasn't afraid to take risks and live through the consequences.

"One day, I decided it was time to become an adult, so I got a job. I had gone to college and graduated late, at age 24. Inside me was a mental clock that told me it was time to go to work and stop being a kid." He made a decision and did what anyone looking for a job in Los Angeles would do in the 1960s: open the *Los Angeles Times* and check out the classified "Help Wanted" ads. He applied to a few jobs and eventually got hired by Mobil Oil as a rep's assistant. It was an indoor desk job, and Bill hated being inside all day. For his next job, Bill started selling copier machines for 3M. "They gave me a car," Bill said, "and a business card, and I really liked being out of the office and on the road." Bill worked for 3M for three years which, for sales reps in that business, was a rarity. Most people didn't stick it out.

You never know when an opportunity will present itself, and for Bill, it happened at a friend's wedding. "I was in the wedding party, and one of the other guys in the party, named Jim Hammond, who worked for Coldwell Banker, and I got to talking candidly about work. He was my age, and he said a lot of guys who are selling copiers are getting into commercial real estate. I asked him, 'How much money can you make doing that?' At the time, I was married, and we were expecting our second child. I told him I made $18,000 a year working for 3M."

"Well, I made fifty grand last year," Jim replied. What? This was a big opportunity.

After a long series of interviews, Bill got a job with Coldwell Banker in Century City. Trouble was, Bill had just bought a home in Orange County, and that commute just wasn't going to work. After trying and failing to get hired at an office closer to home, Bill adjusted. "I noticed Grubb & Ellis had a commercial real estate office near my house. So I interviewed with them. And, guess what? They hired me. I gave my notice at 3M and went home to tell my wife the good news. She asked what the salary was, and I told her there was no salary. It was all commission, a big risk with a new house and only three or four months' worth of money in the bank."

Daring is so much a part of Bill's story. But also important to his story is that he always "made his way" through life from the time he was a kid. He would try something, learn all he could, adjust and ultimately figure it out.

DOLLY PARTON SAYS:

"If you don't like the road you're walking, start paving another one."

That gave him confidence in his new position and in virtually everything else he ever did in life. Bill knew all he had to do was get out on the street and meet people, so that's what he did, and started to score not only a few real estate deals but also countless, often funny, stories to tell. They are memorialized in the book that Bill and I co-wrote, called *Chasing Excellence*, a fabulous read that brings out the best of Bill's Fantastic Life journey, including one about selling copiers that alone is worth the price of the book.

A milestone moment in Bill's story happened about five years into his tenure with Grubb & Ellis. He was asked to represent the brokers as the only representative on the company board. "I went to about five quarterly board meetings," Bill said. "What started to be obvious is that the board didn't really care about the brokers at all. They just cared about shareholder value and building it up. It was terribly disappointing." Bill, being the risk taker, confident in his abilities, able to adjust and make his way through just about anything, began talking to some of the key sales guys about starting their own company. This proved to be one of Bill's hardest sales because even though people were unhappy, they didn't want to walk away from commissions or risk change.

Bill persisted because he felt that the salespeople in a commercial real estate company are the most important people of all. Their needs should be a top priority, and they should have the opportunity to share in the success they create. **After several years of unwavering persistence, never letting go of his dream, Bill rounded up a few colleagues and started his own commercial real**

estate company called Lee & Associates in 1979. Bill's idea grew to multiple offices in California, eventually expanding nationwide.

"I had spent my life taking risks and learning all I could about whatever I was doing. I think if you're going to be successful in selling, and everyone is selling something, you need two things: self-confidence and knowledge. I had a love affair with learning and with real estate." This is what can come from someone whose mind was always wandering, always open to ideas and then making his own decisions to follow them or not. Sometimes it was the decision to ditch school; other times to go out for football. Other times it was jumping from 3M job security to a straight commission sales position and ultimately making the decision to start Lee & Associates.

Bill's story demonstrates how the guy with ADD and lots of ideas can use that story to create the other stories you just heard. Bill's inner voice embraced his abilities and didn't think of them as shortcomings. He didn't beat himself up about not being a good student. Instead, he embraced his gifts and used them to build a Fantastic career that changed the industry and thousands of people's lives.

S<small>TEPHEN</small> C<small>OVEY</small> <small>SAYS</small>: "I am not a product of my circumstances. I am a product of my decisions."

Steps You Can Take

Now it's time for you to consider *your* stories. The ones *you're* living now and the stories in your head. The goal is to envision the future story you want to tell and to maybe assign new meaning to the stories you have been telling yourself for years.

**When you write down
your stories you might hear
something like this from yourself:**

I'm tired. I just need to sleep a little more.
I can work out tomorrow.
They don't know how hard I work.
Why does this always happen to me?

Or maybe it's these...
I can do this.
I rock!
Yes!
It was great.

1
Know Your Stories

First, analyze the present Get real and write down what your stories are right now, and keep writing. You will be analyzing all the stories—the good, the bad, and the ugly. Do it in the daytime and include who you are, what you do, your life circumstances, your wins, your losses, and your truths. What do you tell yourself throughout the day as you wake up, live your current life, and as you go to bed? Get ultra-real and do the same thing in the middle of the night when you can't sleep and hear the stories that are keeping you awake. What are they saying? What's troubling you? Why are they invading your Fantastic Life? Ask yourself, is it fear, doubt, confusion? And when you identify that, ask yourself what are you afraid of, in doubt of, or confused about? Write it all down, and you'll discover the stories that are holding you back from your Fantastic Life. Once you know these stories, you can rewrite them just like John, Robert, and Bill did their Fantastic Lives. There is power in perspective. This is an ongoing exercise. Some stories don't come up for months or even longer. You may find a story that only arises when you are with certain people or in a specific situation. The key is to become aware of the stories you tell yourself. Then make them work for you.

1
Know Your Stories

Look into the future Dare to dream what a Fantastic Life looks and feels like to you. Consider all aspects of your life. Personal self, family, children, business, spiritual, athletic, financial, and more. Be as specific as you can, with no limits. Don't worry about how impossible some of those Fantastic dreams may seem. The "how" doesn't matter. It's the "what" at this stage that really counts. Take the next month and simply listen to yourself. Listen to the stories you tell yourself, then write them down. Get in that habit of catching yourself.

Many times, I find people are so programmed into their current stories and reality that they have forgotten how to dream. The best remedy for that illness is to be bold and let yourself have a dream, even if it will seem small in retrospect. Just allow yourself the possibility of some aspect of your life becoming Fantastic. It might be as simple as getting a new apartment. Or finding a more rewarding job. It might be volunteering in your community or joining a club to meet new people. It might be moving somewhere you've always wanted to live or even just vacationing there. Dream it and write it down as vividly as you can. Write all your dreams down.

1

Know Your Stories

Find all the disconnects Now, look at your future and your present—your stories. Where are the gaps? What aspects of your internal stories are holding you back? Do they stem from your own storyteller voice or the storyteller voices of others? Are they from a long time ago or some incident you don't even think about anymore? One of my stories is from high school. My car (that I bought with my own earnings) got a bent rim on the tire. I had no money to buy a replacement. So my car sat for two weeks until I made some more money. I told myself at that time, and have told myself thousands of times over the last 40 years, "that will never happen again. I will never run out of money." This has driven me to financial freedom. Crazy, but this one story fueled my drive to financially succeed.

Begin reshaping your stories Many of the Rules in this book, when followed, will help you reshape your stories. But, right now, start with one thing you want to change. Maybe part of your future Fantastic Life is traveling to foreign countries. But your story is, "I'm so busy that I'll never be able to take two weeks off to do an overseas vacation." So right now, look at your current state and figure out how you can begin to free up time so that—set a deadline—next year at this time, you'll have a vacation planned and the freedom to take it. Change your story by taking action, and the story in your head will change too. Of all your stories, what's one thing you'd like to reshape or reframe? What's your plan for reshaping that one thing? Then review, refine and repeat for your other stories, writing it all down.

1
Know Your Stories

Memorialize a new beginning ▌│ Keep visible your Future Fantastic stories that you want to live. Read them often. Say them out loud. Check in. Then, keep in your daily view the one thing you are working on changing and your plan for changing it. Schedule into your day consistently, a small block of time to make progress. Not only will this take you where you want to go, but you'll begin developing the habits you'll need to get there.

Yours is a living series of stories, and you're always working on them. Make this work a positive, active force for living your Fantastic Life.

1 | Know Your Stories

Thoughts

- What parts of your story have others defined for you?

- Which ones have you defined for yourself?

- Are you happy with the answers to those two questions, or are they limiting you?

- Have you ever thought about your legacy? Why not write down what you'd like it to be?

- What do you want? What stories do you have that will take you in that direction? Which stories are holding you back? Refine them. This is your Fantastic Life. Let your stories show you the way.

1
Know Your Stories

the FANTASTIC LIFE revisited

As you make your way through life, what you want might change.

Actually, it will change.

Fantastic Life Rule
Be Crystal Clear on What You Want

In Rule #1, you learned how Lee & Associates began from an idea in the wandering mind of a confident, life-long learner named Bill Lee. Years later, the opportunity to open up a Lee office in Arizona presented itself. I, along with several other guys, jumped at the chance, and life got really busy, really fast. I had no idea what I was in for, and the demands of being a founding partner in a start-up business were quickly overtaking every other aspect of my life. Balancing my role as a husband and a new dad, doing the other activities I loved while giving most of my waking hours to this new beast called Lee & Associates all at once seemed impossible. Or so I thought.

Let's be clear; I loved working. Starting a commercial real estate brokerage firm was exciting, challenging, and rewarding. Like the founders of most new businesses, I was doing everything myself, along with my partners. Helping manage the company, hiring people, networking, writing proposals, chasing deals, negotiating contracts, handling the details, closing deals... It was too much. Literally, I would wake up at 3:00 am to work out and head into the office six days a week. I did that for twenty-five years.

Some people might have accepted the fact that they bought the farm, and their only choice was to milk the cows every day. Forever. Others, may not have given their all and failed. Some might have just quit, leaving behind some pretty angry cows and a poor farmer. None of those options were acceptable to me. I liked what I was doing, and it was a means to a bigger end goal I had in mind.

Even at that stage of my life, before I had formulated the idea of The Fantastic Life, I just felt that there had to be a way to do all the things I valued in life at the same time. Family, hobbies, and work. "Do them all." I thought, "This is possible. It just will take me being crystal clear on what I want and having a plan." I got involved with Strategic Coach and its founder Dan Sullivan. Through his program, I evaluated my life, took a good look at what I really wanted at that moment and developed a plan that paved the way to get me there. This plan took decades to make come true, but it was all worth it.

Clarity Isn't Static

Initially, when I was involved in starting the Phoenix Lee & Associates Arizona office, I was crystal clear on what I wanted for my career and my family. They came together perfectly. I wanted a career as a top national commercial real estate broker. I wanted to win at a business that I owned. I also wanted my growing family to live a good life, and my kids to go to good schools and have financial freedom at some point in the future. I was willing to work those long hours, week after week, year after year, to get all that. Let me say, neither success nor freedom came quickly, that's for sure. So I had to figure out how to still do the things I loved, which, at the time, included training for and running ultra-marathons like the Marathon des Sables. It was a time-intensive, seven-day-a-week, highly disciplined process. If you're wondering how I did it, you're reading the guidebook.

The reason I'm telling you this, though, is to point out this fact: As you make your way through life, what you want might change. Actually, it will change. Over time, my drive for success and a balanced life never changed, but what did evolve were my interests. After I ran my sixtieth marathon and ultra-marathon, I realized I was just entering these races to knock them out and check the box. "Yep, done! Next..." I realized I wasn't having fun anymore. What I wanted in life had changed, and I had to accept it and let it go. That was me being crystal clear on what I wanted. I had to admit that I didn't want to run marathons or ultra-marathons anymore. That opened the door for me to take my Tae Kwon Do practice to the ultimate level.

I've seen too many people who spend their whole lives working at a job—or running marathons—because it's what they've always done. Then years go by, and they look back and wonder why they didn't just stop, change things up and go after something else they really wanted. Instead of having fun, they endured life doing

Most people think MONEY will make them happy. When in reality, BEING HAPPY will make you money.

the same old things. They didn't allow themselves to have clarity about what they wanted. They didn't allow their wants to change over time.

My hiking buddy, Brad, and I had set a goal in 2011 that we were going to hike the Pacific Coast Trail (PCT), which runs from Mexico to Canada. After spending a good bit of time researching it and figuring out all the logistics to cover the many legs of the trail, some really remote, I realized, that hiking the more than 2,600-mile-long trail would consume a major portion of my life over the next ten years. I had to ask myself if I was willing to do all it would take to check this accomplishment off my list. Eventually, Brad and I came to the realization that we preferred trekking in more pristine areas, often with no trail. The PCT was not that. So this year, when I made my goal list, hiking the PCT did not make the cut, for the first time in ten years. It was no longer what I wanted.

That's why I get so charged about setting big rock goals, which we'll talk more about later. **Big *rock* goals, when done right, help you crystallize what you really want.** If you want to be a marathon runner, set a big rock goal to run your first race twelve months from now. If you want to own a Ferrari, set a goal to buy one in five years and lay out a plan to afford it. If you want to be able to coach your kids when they get into sports (that was me), set a big rock goal and lay out a plan to make it happen (that was me too).

Know When to Move On

My friend and business associate, Michelle Heeb, is a living example of what I'm talking about. Had Michelle not been crystal clear on what she wanted and brave enough to make changes when needed, she would not be where she is today as founder and owner of Forward Tilt, a cutting-edge office furniture and design company. **Michelle's story drives home the point — when you know what you want, it can be yours, even when there are hurdles and challenges along the way.** Actually, we live a Fantastic Life because there are hurdles and challenges. When overcome, these setbacks add to our confidence and perseverance, much like you heard in Bill Lee's story.

Michelle was born in Detroit, Michigan, of a German mother and an American father who met during the Vietnam war, Michelle's family packed up and moved to Arizona when she was just seven years old. Eventually her parents divorced, and Michelle's mother was left to support two children — Michelle and her younger sister. A pattern of courage and strength began to emerge in Michelle, and it stuck. She started working at the age of 14.

By twenty, Michelle ventured out on her own. At the time she already had six years of experience and a good position performing user training for a technology company. That role led to

> **Know your priorities in life; if you don't know what you want, how can you pursue it?**

more responsibility. **"Here I was, just twenty-one and the company owner said he wanted to make me a sales rep,"** Michelle recounts. **"I told the owner, 'I'm not a salesperson,' to which he promptly replied, 'Yes, you are!'"** That was a major turning point in Michelle's life because ultimately that crossroad uncovered her passion. It illuminated what she really wanted in a career.

How many times does an opportunity present itself, and you shy away thinking, "Hmmm... I don't know how to do that. I might fail," only to regret it later? I hope not very often. Let's make sure it's never after you begin following the rules for living your Fantastic Life. Michelle was brave enough to take on the sales role, something she didn't think she could do. But, she excelled, just as the company owner thought she would. What started to become crystal clear to Michelle is that she enjoyed selling and the feeling of success that it gave her. She was able to focus her inner "hard worker" and use her courageous spirt to achieve more and more.

Still, something was missing. A career in technology was good, but it wasn't the be all, end all for Michelle. That's why when an opportunity in the office furniture industry presented itself, she considered it. The position involved representing several furniture lines in the western U.S. and other nationwide markets. Her courageous spirit kicked in, and she took the job that was big on responsibility and even bigger on potential. Possessing the powerful combination of experienced salesperson and hard worker, Michelle started to see that this position was making her a national expert in office furniture solutions. She was quickly becoming a leader in the field.

Michelle arrived at true clarity when she realized what she liked most about her job was creating inspired workspaces. "The majority of people spend their days working. " Michelle said. "I love making sure that the spaces they are working in are ideal environments. I also love building teams that help accomplish that." She became crystal clear on what she wanted professionally and eventually started her own company to do it. That company is Forward Tilt.

Michelle believes the key is loving what you do. And she says, "It's finding that thing that you care about. I didn't start a business to get rich. I started Forward Tilt so that I could do this important creative work the way, in my heart, I knew it needed to be done. I couldn't do that working for other people who often didn't feel the same sense of purpose I feel." That's clarity. And today, Michelle wakes up excited to go to work. In that way, she is leading a Fantastic Life.

Just as you might expect from a founder and CEO with clear vision, Michelle has ushered Forward Tilt into industry leadership. Unlike most companies in the business, Forward Tilt saw major sales increases during the Covid-19 pandemic when everyone was working from home. Michelle's focus has fueled Forward Tilt, and now that success fuels Michelle's Fantastic Life. She's having fun. That's what happens when you're crystal clear about what you want.

Not everyone gets clarity in life the exact same way Michelle did. It's an individual process, and often clarity comes bit by bit. You may find you like waking up early, enjoy surrounding yourself with people, or prefer working with your hands. Each of these are points of clarity that add up to a broader realization over time. Forcing it doesn't work.

While you are gaining clarity in one area of your life, don't limit advancing other areas of your Fantastic Life. That would be a waste of time and you never know when progress in one area of your life will clarify another. Remember everything is connected. Clarity is not just in your work, but in all areas of your life and at all times of your life. What you want when you are 20, might not be the same thing when you are 30. We are all growing and changing, so your clarity is not forever. Seeking clarity is a lifelong habit to be curated.

Two Types of Fun

Michelle's journey follows a Fantastic Life path because, along the way, she successfully followed Rule number two and came to grips with the reality of her job: She wasn't having fun anymore. Okay, it's true; often you have to get through the grind and pay your dues to achieve your goal. The journey isn't always fun. You'll know the difference because when you're crystal clear on achieving something, you'll pay the price and do the work. Quitting isn't an option.

To that point, did you know there are two types of fun? Type 1 Fun happens in the moment of doing something, like skiing, seeing a movie, or playing with your kids. The second kind of fun happens after you do something, usually something hard, and you sit back and say, "Man, I did it. That was fantastic!" That's how I feel whenever I ride my Peloton bike. The ride itself isn't fun, but it feels so good afterward. It's Type 2 Fun. If you're not experiencing either of these two types of fun, then it's time to get clarity on what is fun, the related goals, and then get busy doing the work.

Steps You Can Take

As you can see, living a Fantastic Life isn't easy, but within it is a lot of fun—both kinds. Tiring perhaps in the moment, yet energizing too. And certainly rewarding with every accomplishment along the way. Living your Fantastic Life is being alive. Here's how you can start to clarify your own life. It's a starting point, and every Fantastic Life has one. No time like the present.

EARL NIGHTINGALE SAYS: "Never give up on a dream just because of the time it will take to accomplish it. The time will pass anyway."

Examine your entire life A lot of people would rather not examine their lives because they are afraid of what they'll find. Will it be depressing? Will they see a life of missed opportunities, a life wasted? Please don't think like that; it's completely the wrong mindset. The way to think about this is "starting today..." and then fill in the blank with what you really want your life to be. But first, you have to see what's happening right now, so you get a clear picture of how you're spending your time. What activities you do at work, at home, with your friends, in the community, and more. Think about how much time you spend at each, and include all the time wasters too. Ask yourself, "Is this something bringing me closer to my goals? Am I experiencing Type 1 or Type 2 Fun? What can I do to make it better?" You'll be surprised how you can capture that time and put it to fantastic use. More on that later!

2

Be Crystal Clear on What You Want

Make a detailed list or journal entry 🔳 Once you see what your life looks like today, broken down, as I suggest previously, you can focus on how you want it to be. You'll also find you have more clarity when opportunities come your way, and you'll discover where you want and need to grow. This exercise delivers some powerful awakenings.

Recognize that you can achieve anything but not everything you want. I always say the best work is done in the context of constraint and intense focus. What that means is that when you limit the scope of what you do and unleash your intensity and focus, your work and your work product both improve. Look at that priority list and all the ideas coming to mind right now that might help you achieve those priorities. Recognize that you can't do them all. You won't have the time, the money, or the energy. That's okay. With your new-found "can't do everything" attitude, you'll make better progress on your priority.

Set your priorities 🔳 Once you have your list, circle the top five priorities. Keep them visible. In the next chapter, I'll tell you more about how you'll use these priorities. These are the things you absolutely want in life. And if you've been working as you've been reading, which I hope you have been, by this point, you should be crystal clear on what you really want. That's great because you'll need that clarity to move forward. If you're not yet clear, go back and break your life down even further. Find pieces of clarity. Your life can be a puzzle, and putting those pieces together (heck, even just finding the pieces) is critical for living a Fantastic Life.

2

Be Crystal Clear on What You Want

Filter your life Start making a plan for how you'll achieve your priorities. As part of that plan, prepare to give up some of the things distracting you from your priorities and the life you really want. Things like spending time on social media (one of the biggest time wasters in today's world, unless it's your job), too many nights out with friends that interfere with your family priorities, or saying, "Yes," to work projects that don't further your career priorities. I know it sucks to think you'll have to stop doing things, but if you are crystal clear on what you want and you are honest, the things you are banishing from your life will be the ones you'll be happy to see go. They likely weren't doing it for you anyway.

2 Be Crystal Clear on What You Want

Thoughts

▌ What is most important to you right now, at this place in your life?

▌ Where are you spending your time and energy?

▌ Is it on things that are important to you?

▌ What are the activities and commitments that are keeping you from focusing on your top five priorities?

▌ Are they important, and if so, why?

▌ How can you cut back or eliminate those things that aren't furthering your priorities?

▌ How can you focus on the things that are furthering your priorities?

▌ How can you schedule your life to live your priorities?

▌ It's time to accept this truth: "How you spend your time is how you spend your life."

2
Be Crystal Clear on What You Want

the FANTASTIC LIFE revisited

When you know your areas of focus precisely, and you plan to make progress in those areas, well, those become your resumes.

Fantastic Life Rule 3
Build Your Resumes Every Year

You might think this chapter goes without saying. "Of course, I'll build my resume every year. Well, maybe not every year. And I might not write it all out, but in any given year, surely I've done something 'resume-worthy' in twelve months if I sat down and thought about it." Ha-ha! That's what you might be thinking, so I hope what I have to say next surprises you. The rule is "Build your resumes," plural, and I'm not suggesting that multiple people build their resumes. I'm suggesting that you build your own multiple resumes.

Multiple resumes? Yes, because when you commit to living a Fantastic Life, you commit to achieving in areas beyond your professional life. Remember my "balance" story a few pages ago? A Fantastic Life is setting, working toward, and achieving goals in every important area of your life all at once. Because as you are coming to learn in this book, a Fantastic Life means you have learned how to make room in your life for all the things you want to do. So naturally, you'll be building your resumes—all of them—consistently, every day, week, month, and year. Of course, there is a method to this madness.

You may know people who seem to accomplish more than the average person. So much more than most people, in fact, that you might wonder, "How in the heck do they do it? They don't have any more hours in the day than I do." In truth, though, they do have more time because they create more time. They have mastered and now practice the Rules in this book, some of which are Rules that help you determine what you want and others that show you how to get it done.

For the sake of explaining this Rule, let's assume you're going to accomplish a lot in the coming months. We'll assume you'll be crystal clear about what you want, and you'll have a game plan for getting there (see Rule #6 Set Goals), in multiple areas of your life. Big assumptions, I know, but you will get there once you sit down and start working through this book. The resumes then that you will build after reading this chapter —you'll need one for each of the important areas of your life—will be your beginning benchmark for a lifetime of Fantastic entries in the years to follow. So don't worry if one or more of your resumes is pretty scant and others are really jam-packed. That's part of the process, part of the awakening, "Wow! I need to pay more attention to this area of my life and accomplish more. I gotta do something about that."

Your Resumes

If you're wondering what resumes you should have and the categories you should include, just think back to the previous chapter about being crystal clear on what you want. When you know your areas of focus precisely and plan to progress in those areas, well, those become your resumes. In general, I believe everyone should have three to six resumes. Here are the most common:

Professional This is your typical work resume that includes experiences, education, skills, and positions held. Add to it professional awards, milestone projects you're proud of, meaningful relationships you've formed, big clients you've landed, etc.

Personal This is your personal development resume. It includes everything you're doing for your own mental, physical, and emotional well-being. So you can see right there categories that might make great homes for workshops you've attended, books you've read, hiring and learning from coaches, and mentors, your meditation practice, diet, etc.

Athletic Your athletic resume includes all your fitness accomplishments, like your current training level and new activities and progress. If you are competitive, include your races, your finishing times, your games and team standing, etc. I categorize my athletic resume by sport.

Family It's important to have a family resume, given that the roles we play in a family are so vital to our well-being and the well-being of others. You might set goals around your role as a spouse or partner, your role as a parent and for child rearing, your role as a son or daughter who takes care of and spends time with aging parents, your role as a provider, your role in having fun and taking family vacations, etc.

Community This resume covers all your civic posts, your volunteerism, your charitable giving, leadership positions, etc. Often people have tithing or giving goals for the year, and that's great. But why not also have participation goals so you can share your talents too?

Spiritual A large number of people lead their lives spiritually. If that's you, your spiritual resume will likely grow each year. You may discover, as I have, that this resume can be one of the most rewarding to build.

These are just some examples of resumes you may want to build. **Your resumes need to cover the most important areas of your life** and be general enough so you won't get bogged down in which achievement goes where. Why do we spend our days busying ourselves with all these things, all these goals, and tasks? Why work out? Why hire a personal trainer? Why read books that help us understand ourselves and others? Why attend workshops and seminars to learn new skills? Why meditate? Why, why, why? The answer is, first and foremost, because a Fantastic Life is a meaningful life. A life filled with consistent growth, learning, improvement, and accomplishments in the most important areas of your life. And building your resumes is a way to do just that. This is Type 2 fun. A lot of growth comes from Type 2 Fun.

We also take on tasks and projects so that we can do other things we either love to do or must do to go forward in life. I love this quote by T. Harv Eker: "If you are willing to do only what's easy, life will be hard. But if you're willing to do what's hard, life will be easy." Here's a great example. I'm not a young guy, but I built a morning routine where every day, I do push-ups when I wake up. Right in my closet. Nearly every day, I hike or ride the Peloton bike. And yes, I stay in good shape. Why do I do that? First and foremost, it makes everything else I love to do easier. From hanging out and keeping up with my adult kids, to spending thirty nights a year backpacking and sleeping on the ground in the wilderness, to walking for hours, taking in the sites on vacations with my wife and kids. And yes, doing the tasks I have to do for my job.

The last time I was in Las Vegas on business, I had to do site tours of commercial buildings. There were a bunch of us and we rented a van. Let's face it, no one wants to crawl to that back, back seat. "I'll jump in the far back," I said, Now, while I was the oldest guy in the group, I was fine sitting in the way back and frankly had the most agility to drop down low and crawl into and out of the cramped back seat twenty-five times in the span of the day. How come I could do that? Because I work on

T. HARV EKER SAYS: "If you are willing to do only what's easy, life will be hard. But if you're willing to do what's hard, life will be easy."

my athletic resume consistently every day. Now, this is a tiny example, but it is a meaningful one. How many things in your life could be easier if you were more fit? How many things would you love to be doing that you're not because you don't think you can?

Why Resumes are Important

There are so many reasons why I love working with people and sharing the importance of building their resumes. First, **resumes will show you the things you are not working toward but are important to you.** If these are the most important areas of your life, and you're missing out on a few, are you living your priorities? **Resumes can also vividly show you the things you have always wanted to do.** If the only entries on your athletic resume are from fifteen years ago and you've always wanted to run a 10K, well, then, that says something. What are you doing in your daily life that could be replaced with training for a 10K? Maybe you don't want it that bad.

My hiking buddy, Brad, and I have done and continue to do some really cool hikes, like a 20-mile loop up Humphrey's Peak in Flagstaff, Arizona, the highest peak in Arizona at 12,637 feet. Not a huge deal for experienced hikers like us, except that we did it while fasting for 48 hours. We joke because we normalize, yes, normalize, these kinds of activities that seem extreme to other people. As you begin building your resumes, you'll see the things you normalize in your life, the things you make part of your normal activities.

Here's a trick: look at what you have normalized in your life and decide if you are happy with that or if maybe it is time to push for a new normal. The new normal might be something that goes on your resume. Substitute four hours of television a night with a bike ride. Make the bike ride the new normal and add it to your resume. Then as you increase your rides, time, and distance, update your resume. It's that easy.

The second reason I preach resumes is because having multiple resumes can help you see vividly that one area of your life might be using up the majority of your energy at the expense of all other areas of your life. Yes, there are times when this is bound to happen, like when you start a company, you have a baby, or you train for a triathlon. In those periods of intense focus, this is entirely understandable, but it should not be the norm.

That was my story when I started my company—work was taking over everything. So I looked at my not-so-fantastic reality and took steps to normalize adding a marathon training schedule to my life. Recognize that an object in motion tends to stay in motion. You probably learned

WHY ARE RESUMES SO IMPORTANT?

1. Resumes show you if you're not working toward something important to you.
2. Resumes show you if one area of your life is overtaking the others.
3. Resumes give you something to look back on and say "Wow!"
4. Building resumes is super motivating.

that in high school physics class. So if you are in motion continually with work, you may be caught in Newton's Law. When one of your resumes is pages long, and others are little more than a page title, well... it may be time to focus on other areas.

I created a concept I call "Rolling Start" when I find I am focused too much on one or two resumes. Here's how it works. To grow different resumes, I look at each one to find small, doable ways I can get a rolling start on progress. Just a small step from which I can build greater momentum. Here are a couple of ideas for each resume:

Professional
- » Sign up for a seminar
- » Learn a new technology

Personal
- » Read two pages of a book a day – every day
- » Create an evening meditation routine

Athletic
- » Create a morning routine
- » Do push-ups between business calls or Zoom meetings

Family
- » Have one family meal a week
- » Call your parents on Sundays

Community
- » Become a mentor
- » Volunteer at a Boys & Girls Club

Spiritual
- » Order a spiritual book and start reading two pages a day
- » Buy a spiritual inspiration calendar or download an app

One huge way to get time back is to give up social media. For many people, with this one Fantastic Life-altering change, you can have enough time to build each of your resumes. So if you are an object in motion in only one area of your life, experiment with these Rolling Start ideas and get into motion in other areas too.

The third reason why I'm such a fan of multiple resumes is because as you start focusing on and creating your Fantastic Life, **you'll look back on your resumes and think, "I did all that? I can't believe it. I've become one of those people who seem to have more hours in the day than everyone else**! I've normalized a daily run, or cooking a healthy dinner every night, or studying a foreign language for an hour a day." Whatever it is, it belongs on your resume. Others will notice your accomplishments and think you're amazing too. They'll wonder how you seem to have more hours in the day than they do, how you seem to be doing so much more, and how you manage to live such a Fantastic Life.

Finally, the last reason is because these resumes and building them are super motivating. **Once you get started, believe me, you'll want to keep going, want to keep adding to your resume, and seeing your progress. And in the process, guess what? You're living the Fantastic Life.** It's a full, rich and exciting journey that would remain hidden if not for the resumes. They open your eyes initially to your priorities, they give you a framework to document your progress at the 30,000-foot level, and they give you the drive to keep going. Look how far you've come! That's the power of the resumes.

Resumes Deliver Impact

When I think of building multiple resumes and the impact that mindset can have on your life and the lives of others around you, one name comes to mind: Sharon Harper. Let me tell you about Sharon.

Sharon has multiple resumes in her highly accomplished life. Truly I've never met a person who can move mountains quite like Sharon and impact so many people positively in the process. Sharon's resumes include accomplishments in terms of her professional career, her charitable giving, her civic participation, and of course, her family.

Speaking of family, Sharon raised four children, plus one niece. Sharon and her husband spent decades raising these young people—who are now productive and successful young adults—to recognize the importance of goal setting, of achievement of volunteerism, and of doing well by doing good. Sharon and her husband have modeled all those things, witnessed by their entries on their resumes.

"Building my resumes every year is just something I naturally do," said Sharon when I spoke with her about this Fantastic Life Rule. "I always have a lot going on." Sharon co-founded a real estate development company forty years ago called Plaza Companies. Today it is a much bigger firm, and they are the leader in development of healthcare, bio-sciences, mixed-use projects, senior housing, and more. They also own vertical businesses in construction, property management, and all the back-of-house support. "We're a company that can take on another developer's project or build from the ground up. And we've been on the forefront of a number of significant public and private partnerships with universities and municipalities."

There's No End to What You Can Accomplish

Sharon's impressive professional resume includes being the master developer for SkySong, the Arizona State University (ASU) Innovation Center, and developing the Banner Estrella Medical Center, Creighton University Health Sciences Campus, and many award-winning senior living communities. You might believe that because of the professional responsibilities that come with projects of that caliber, Sharon wouldn't have a moment to do anything else except work. Not so. Her community leadership reaches far and wide, and there are simply too many board positions, chairmanships, and appointments to list them all, but here are a diverse few: Valley Leadership Woman of the Year, Honorary Commander of Luke Air Force Base, Board of Governors for TGen, Most Admired Leader by the Phoenix Business Journal, ASU Board of Trustees, Trustee for the Virginia G. Piper Charitable Trust, Trustee for Creighton University, Sandra Day and John O'Connor Award for Outstanding Community Service, and dozens more.

Not every one of your resumes will have A+ accomplishments every year.

Sharon is also the most humble person I know, but she is the first to say, **"Every year, we take a quantum leap from what we have done before. I'm always looking forward to the future, new ideas, and new things."** That goes for her company and her civic leadership. Sharon has led presidential, senate, and gubernatorial election campaigns and Arizona's Proposition 123, which brought, as Sharon said, "Five billion, with a B, dollars to Arizona schools."

Sharon's civic resume has had an immense impact in the Southwest, the nation, and even the world. Her efforts also impact her children and grandchildren, who have grown up normalized to making a difference in the community. Being involved is their normal.

Her daughter is a frontline physician at Banner Health, the largest hospital network in Arizona. When Sharon learned that during the COVID-19 pandemic, they were using the same masks for three days at a time, she decided to figure out how to get enough supplies to Arizona. "Everyone was trying—the governor's office, the White House, the military—but no one was successful," Sharon said. Through partnerships with foreign countries that Sharon orchestrated, 11 million masks were shipped to Arizona and distributed to first responders, caregivers, and frontline workers at eighty hospitals in every corner of the state. "I wanted our community to be safe," Sharon said.

In August 2021, when the Afghanistan evacuation needed urgent help, Sharon stepped up to assist in the evacuation of 167 young women, many who relocated to Arizona and have now successfully enrolled at ASU.

Sharon drove home the point of Rule #3, building your resume every year when she paused and thought for a moment and said, "I'm always thinking about what's next. And then, I give it a shot." What's next... give it a shot. Those two phrases have saved lives, made lives, and continue to move mountains.

As you think of your resumes and building them, think about what's next. What is your next goal or your next step in achieving a goal? Then just give it a shot. So simple and so powerful. My guess is that when you start thinking and acting on these words, your resumes will begin filling up in no time flat.

Steps You Can Take

Here are some ways you can put to work the things we've talked about in this chapter. They will set the stage for everything else you do in your Fantastic Life and help you with all the other Rules.

"Some people live 90 years; others live one year 90 times."

Treat your whole life like you do your work
While in the throes of your daily life, it's all too easy to forget that all life is connected. Sometimes you give your all in one area, like work, and then slack off on other areas because you're just burned out or maybe no longer interested in something you used to enjoy. If you've lost interest in something, it might be time to get crystal clear on what you want. But if you are neglecting just one area of your life, you'll find that shortfall will start impacting the other areas, too. When approaching your goals for your other resumes, yes, be realistic, and then go for achieving those goals as you would a goal at work.

Determine what things are the most important in your life That's how you'll know what resumes you need to create. If you have worked through the first few chapters of this book, what is important to you should be obvious. If you have not yet done the work of Rules #1 and #2, you may want to do it now.

Build Your Resumes Every Year

Build and manage your multiple resumes In this chapter, I've given you suggestions for your resumes. You can create others if they work better for you. Most important, however, is to know that your resumes are not something you create and put in a drawer somewhere and forget about them. No, you'll want to have them available so you can review and update them often. At least every year, take time to review not just your work resume but all your resumes. Add to them if you haven't already. See where you succeeded and where you missed. Ask yourself why. And then answer the question honestly. Maybe you are no longer interested in that goal. I had "learning to fly a plane" as one of my goals for years. One year, after making no real progress, again, I looked at it and said, "Yeah, I guess I don't really want to learn to fly that bad." I took it off the list. Perfectly fine. And that's the point. Reassess every year and adjust your goals.

Consider life as a journey, not a destination Particularly, the Fantastic Life is a journey. Each resume is a visible, material way to make sure you keep growing. There is no stopping point in life. Stopping is truly how people wither away and die. The resume mindset keeps you focused on the truth that there is no end, no real destination. And the more you accomplish, the more you'll see what you have yet to do, the more ways you can grow. That's how I see it. Each milestone creates new opportunities, new adventures, and new discoveries. When you think and take action with your six resumes, you will accomplish more in the next three years, or even one or two years, than you could ever imagine.

3. Build Your Resumes Every Year

Thoughts

▌ What are the most important things to you in life?

▌ What things do you let distract you from those priorities?

▌ What are the things you really, really want to accomplish?

▌ How realistic are they, and what do you need?

▌ What significant achievements have you had in the last year?

▌ Have you accomplished all you have set out to do?

▌ Why? Or why not?

▌ What small step/action/habit will give you a Rolling Start for each resume?

Build Your Resumes Every Year

the FANTASTIC LIFE® revisited

Let's get to the heart
of this by asking yourself
one very important question:
"Where can I win?"
It really is that simple.

Fantastic Life Rule

Play Where You Can Win

The last chapter was about building resumes, multiple resumes, for the important areas of your life. It isn't about seeing who can amass the longest lists. Rather, the resumes help you recognize your big wins, reflect on what it took to get those wins, and bask in that Fantastic feeling of achievement. They also tell you where you need to go to work.

When you look at your resumes, you may see a pattern in your wins. For example, on my athletic resume, I have many accomplishments from running marathons and hiking remote terrain, but I don't have any accomplishments in playing golf or tennis. That's because I play where I can win.

When you play where you can win, you'll find you can achieve more, and the path is often more enjoyable. It might not be any easier, but at least you're working with, not against, your strengths, which gives you more confidence for the next thing you do. After all, what good is building your resumes with accomplishments that were so grueling and unsatisfying that you would never want to do them again? What's the point of that? It's certainly not a Fantastic Life.

A Fantastic Life is one where even the hard stuff is worthwhile and, dare I say, enjoyable because you get that second kind of fun, that Fantastic feeling of accomplishment. Let's get to the heart of this by asking yourself one fundamental question: "Where can I win?" It really is that simple. If, for instance, you want to take your business international and you have connections in England, start there. It's a place where you can win. If you have no connections in Japan, maybe don't start there. It will be harder than it would be in England to get the wins that will keep you going.

I know this seems obvious, but it isn't. I see people all the time in the wrong place, in the wrong job, in the wrong company in terms of their strengths. It's so easy to get caught up in sub-optimal situations and not know how to get out or be too afraid to get out. But here's a first step. **Living a Fantastic Life means constantly asking, "Am I in the right place to get a win?" And if not, what can I do to put myself in the right place at the right time?** Which is what this chapter is about.

In a later chapter, we'll cover another question to ask yourself: "Will I take my shot in this place and this time to get a win?" A Fantastic Life is putting yourself in the right place and then going for the win. At this moment, can you honestly say that you are both in the right place and willing to go for the win? If yes, keep reading. If not, you may want to ask yourself why. What is off in your world?

Be In the Right Place

After my senior year of college, the Minnesota Twins drafted me to play professional baseball. I was a pretty good player, and they saw some raw talent they felt they could develop in the farm system. It was a rush being part of professional baseball. It was also a ticket to being poor. Playing minor league baseball doesn't pay much, and I had way loftier financial goals for myself and my future. If I could get to the majors, no problem. I'd play ball and make a lot of dough. The problem was, I came to realize I wasn't going to get there. Major league baseball wasn't a place where I could win. I had the drive; I just didn't have enough talent for the sport at that level. So, I didn't keep dreaming, hoping, and wasting time. I got out and found a place where I could win.

That place was 100% commission-based commercial real estate, a highly competitive and lucrative business. I didn't know it at the time, but it turned out that my personality, talent, and drive were perfect for this work, which felt more like a new competitive sport to me than a business. It was perfect. I wanted to put myself where it was up to me to be successful. I wanted to bet on my drive, my focus, and my work ethic. Showing up early, making cold calls, and then more cold calls, landing an appointment, doing the research, showing properties, negotiating deals, making more cold calls, and working seventy to eighty hours a week for decades to

VINCE LOMBARDI SAYS:

"Winning isn't everything, but wanting to win is."

build a business for myself and my young family. It was like training camp, batting practice, and strength training. Over time, I began winning.

But how many people don't play where they can win? They are afraid to move to a different city even though they hate the one they're in. Or they stick with the same company, hoping and praying, even though they know advancing is unlikely. They're in jobs they hate. They're doing work that doesn't challenge them. They aren't meeting people who can take them further in their careers. None of these are places they can win.

Status Quo or Being Bold Are Choices

Maybe I'm talking about you. You have goals, and maybe the chair you're sitting in from sun up to sun down will never take flight and let you soar to the heights of your dreams. Or maybe it's a chair that could take you to new heights, but you're just not the right pilot. Or perhaps those aren't the heights you dream of attaining. We have all been in one or all of these circumstances, and they pretty much suck. You can be bold and make a move or stay where you are, sucking it up, hoping, and enduring.

What is playing where you can win? Consistently evaluating your skills, your natural abilities, and your relationships and aligning them with opportunities that are available to you. If you want something that does not fit your current skills, go get new skills! If you want a new career, but don't know anyone, go make new relationships. If you think you can do better, plan your attack and execute.

Too many people have "a job." And that job leaves them empty. Why is that? Because that job is not a place where they can win. And by win, I mean scoring little wins, too. Not just big ones. Small wins matter, maybe more than the big wins, because if they happen frequently enough in your day, they can make for a pretty Fantastic day. String a bunch of Fantastic days together, and you have a Fantastic Life.

Ever hear people say, "Yeah, I wasn't 'cut out' for the job?" What they're saying is, "Yeah, I wasn't playing where I could win. I thought I was, but it turns out I wasn't." Again, they are not bad people, just not playing where they can win. It happens all the time. Where in your life are you playing where you can win? Where are you not?

> You can be bold and make a move or stay where you are, sucking it up, hoping, and enduring.

See Reality

I love the quote by Jack Welch, former CEO of GE. He said, "Face reality as it is... not as you wish it to be." How true is that? Now, see yourself for who you are, not who you wish you were. If you don't like who you are or where you are, change it. You can! First, face reality as it is, not how you wish it to be. Second, strategize. Third, execute.

Here's another example. Ever wonder what the turnover rate is for telemarketing? Statistics show that the average call center replaces 30 to 40 percent of its workers every year. In some centers, that number is as high as 100 percent. In a single year! If you don't have a personality that can take getting hung up on 200 times a day, then don't take that job. It's not a place where you can win. You'll be miserable, and your life will be far less than Fantastic.

Again, certain people may be able to succeed in that environment. But many won't, and yet, they take the job anyway, knowing what's involved. Then they hate their work and workplace, complain, and wonder why their life isn't Fantastic and basically sucks. They're miserable because they made a choice to play where they couldn't possibly win.

Now, if you have a goal and want to be successful, you need to gut it out and do a solid year of cold calling to put you where you can win, then I say go for it. Life is putting yourself in a position to win; sometimes it takes a few intermediate steps. Steps that may not be very fantastic at the moment, but that will take you where you want to go.

Find and Use Your Strengths

Michael Welborn, one of my long-time friends and colleagues, has had a stellar career playing where he can win even though, as he said, "I always got jobs I wasn't qualified for." Among them, Mike has held chairman, CEO, and president titles in banking, restaurants, mortgage lending, and healthcare, a diverse mix of companies and industries. He also led high-profile Arizona initiatives like getting a new stadium built for the Arizona Cardinals, which added wins in politics, sports, development, and construction to his resume. Either Mike can win in a lot of places, or there's something more to his story. And there is.

It turns out "play where you can win" applies to more than just cities, sports, companies, and jobs. It has more to do with your natural talents, even if you don't know exactly what those talents are. Often, others see something in us we don't see in ourselves, and that has been the case with Mike many times over.

Mike spent much of his career in banking— he was the president of a major mortgage company at the young age of 31. "Looking back I knew nothing about anything at that age, but I asked a lot of questions and always built a team of great experienced

JACK WELCH, FORMER CEO OF GE SAYS: "Face reality as it is... not as you wish it to be."

Play Where You Can Win

89 — 4

people," Mike said. But still, he achieved great results. Later, he became the chairman of two Arizona banks and was eventually promoted to a senior position in Chicago, where he suddenly had 30,000 people working for him. "Again, I'm in a position that seemed way out of my league, but there I was." Mike's a humble guy. It wasn't out of his league. He had a "league" within himself that he didn't yet recognize. A place where he could win.

When Mike retired from banking in 2005, he kept getting offers from banks to come work for them. None of those offers intrigued him. But when the very talented CEO of P.F. Chang's China Bistro knocked on his door and said, "Why don't you come work for us. You can do all the stuff I don't want to do," it seemed perfect.

Mike described it as a very successful $800 million company, yet being run like a smaller company. "I knew that wasn't sustainable. So, I helped the company evolve strategy, take on a leadership role, and scale their brands." Those skills were among the commonalities in Mike's career successes. They were places Mike could win.

Eventually, with the company growing, Mike got the idea, "Let's start an international business. Everyone thought I was crazy. It'll never work." But work it did. In short order, P.F. Chang's China Bistro had more than 120 restaurants in

28 countries. His next move? "I thought the brand was ripe to create a line of frozen foods. People thought I was crazy again." He proved the skeptics wrong. That business grew to $150 million before he finally retired from the company.

Malcolm Gladwell's book Outliers made K. Anders Ericsson's research work famous. Ericsson said it takes 10,000 hours of intensive practice to become proficient at something. "Well, I didn't have anything close to that in running restaurants. I had never even worked in a restaurant, so I spent a month waiting tables, washing dishes, bartending, and doing kitchen prep work," Mike admitted.

What Mike did have, however, is tens of thousands of hours clocked in strategy, leadership, and scaling businesses. **Mike worked his strengths even if he wasn't entirely sure what they were.** As long as new opportunities allowed him to use those skills, both he and the companies were set up for big wins. "I don't do well if a company just wants to sit there and not scale. I don't take those opportunities." Mike is on track to create even more wins as the chairman of the board for HonorHealth, one of Arizona's largest healthcare systems.

K. ANDERS ERICSSON SAYS:

"It takes 10,000 hours of intensive practice to become really proficient at something."

the FANTASTIC LIFE® revisited

Become the Strongest

As Mike's career demonstrates, **outstanding accomplishments that bring immense satisfaction, that drive confidence, and set you up for more success come from playing where you can win.** They also come from practicing and doing the work that will make you the strongest. By that, I mean the strongest in the game, your game, whatever that game may be.

Jeff Bezos, in 1990, when he was just thirty years old, worked for a hedge fund in New York and rose through the ranks to become a vice president. In 1994, he shocked everyone and left the firm to found the online bookseller, Amazon, in his garage. Over decades he used his computer, financial, and engineering talent to grow Amazon, bit by bit, and became the most powerful retailer in history.

Richard Branson got his start when he founded his first magazine called Student at age sixteen. After selling $8,000 worth of advertising in the first issue, he dropped out of school to promote the magazine. From there, he started a mail-order record business called Virgin. That was 1972. That company grew into record stores and eventually Virgin Records. Next, it was Virgin Books and Virgin Video. His business empire grew to over fifty different companies with combined sales of $17 million, a rounding error in his world today. In the 1980's he founded Virgin Atlantic, which revolutionized air travel comforts. Branson became the best at innovation by starting small and building from there.

RICHARD BRANSON

Elon Musk's story isn't all that much different. He preceded his launch into space through many far smaller wins. Not long after graduating from Stanford in 1995, Musk and his brother Kimbal founded a company called Zip2 Corporation which provided city guide and directory software to various newspapers. Four years later, Compaq Computer bought the company for $300 million. A big win, but tiny by today's standards for Musk. Rather than retire and live off his wealth, Musk once again played where he could win—transformational businesses—and founded X.com, which eventually became PayPal. He fought the upward battle to make paying online something we take for granted today, the same thing he is doing with Tesla and now with Space X.

ELON MUSK

Look at people like **Jeff Bezos**, **Richard Branson**, and **Elon Musk**, who are by far the strongest players in their own games. Each of them transformed their industries—retail, airlines, cars—and now they are taking on space travel. But before they launched themselves into the stratosphere and beyond, they racked up millions of little wins and became stronger.

Retail, airlines, and engineering are not areas where I can play and win. I don't have the passion for doing the work it would take to be the strongest as I do in commercial real estate. I'm not technical enough, and I'm not sufficiently interested in these industries to dedicate myself to the work. How about you? It's worth thinking about because the kind of passion and interest Bezos, Branson, Musk, and Mike Welborn have are vital to playing where you can win and living a Fantastic Life.

Steps You Can Take

Assess the areas of your life Take a look at the areas of your life where you're putting in the most effort. Is it your job, your hobbies, or your family? Decide if you are working from your strengths or struggling to overcome your weaknesses. Are you in a place to score small or big wins in those arenas?

List what you'd rather be doing This goes back to considering your goals and clarity of purpose. Instead of the environments and tasks occupying your days right now, are there some other place or alternative activities that you wish you were doing instead? What strengths might you have to help you score wins for each?

Be bold Create a plan to exit the areas of your life where you can't win. This will take some courage, but you have to do it. No one ever lived a Fantastic Life by feeling trapped in a winless situation. It is time to be really honest with yourself. And to know that when you find that place where you can win, you will. Believing in that truth will get you where you need to go.

4

Play Where You Can Win

Place yourself where you can win This is all about taking action. Am I saying quit your winless job? Maybe. Or maybe it's moonlighting on that new business idea you want to pursue. When you get some wins, make the leap at your job. Your leap might be moving to a new city. Or even getting a new set of friends with similar aspirations.

Gain clarity. Create a plan. Execute. Eventually, the rubber has to meet the road on this Rule. You have to do the work, plan your next steps and then move forward to get them done. Remember, your steps don't have to be anything drastic. Just spend time playing where you can win. In the next chapter, we'll talk about getting those wins.

4
Play Where You Can Win

99

Thoughts

■ What are you good at?

■ What do you love doing and wish you could do more of?

■ Who can help you discover your strengths?

■ What areas of life are you struggling in because you're not using your strengths?

■ What areas of life are you using your strengths?

■ What must you do to get into more places where you can win?

4

Play Where You Can Win

the **FANTASTIC** LIFE revisited

... any win is a good win.
And when you get a win,
it sets you up for getting
even more wins.

Fantastic Life Rule 5
Get a Win

First of all, let's agree right up front that any win is a good win. And when you get a win, it sets you up for getting even more wins. That's just how the world seems to work. In Rule #4, I challenged you to play where you can win. Whether it is a location, company, sport, job, or skill set, playing in that space sure can help you operate with a winning mindset. And by that, I mean a winning mindset is one where you think about wins throughout your day. Instead of your day's activities being one big blur, how about looking instead at the little wins you score along the way? When you train yourself—your mind, that is—to see all the wins you accomplish and let yourself, your psyche, or your soul, feel the high of those wins, you'll want to do more of them. You'll actually start searching for wins. It's a scientific fact.

I've never been a drug user. Unless you count dopamine, the hormone our bodies naturally secrete when we do an activity like exercising, eating, working, etc. For me, that "activity" might be doing something difficult or that I don't particularly want to do, then grinding through it and recognizing the win on the other side. Instantly, my brain kicks out quantities of dopamine, training my body to feel the Type 2 Fun: the reward, satisfaction, and motivation. Then I crave more. I love that feeling of accomplishment, the dopamine rush, when I get a win. I'm not alone; that cycle is within all of us and is the science behind the importance of scoring and feeling wins.

It's that "mission accomplished" feeling that propels you toward other wins because you want to feel that rush again. Wouldn't it be Fantastic to have more of those in your day and never miss one? Of course, it would. To make sure I get my share in my life, I take the "any win is a good win" mantra to heart by categorizing as wins, countless things others likely overlook. For instance, I think this way during cold call sessions. Getting "a meaningful" is a win. What is "a meaningful?" It is when someone picks up and actually talks to you. That's a win. Here are some big steps in getting wins:

1. **Play where you can win** (See Rule #4)

2. **"Create" wins** This is your Fantastic Life. Count getting out of bed without hitting the snooze button as a win. Taking the time to brush your teeth and use the water-pik. Calling your mother; that's a win. You see what I'm saying. Wins aren't just placing in the top three of an Ironman competition.

3. **Become a "win" machine** From the time you get up to the time you go to bed – focus on and get wins.

I'll warn you, the doing is always hard. But I can promise you, the win will feel Fantastic.

A Win Should Feel Like a Win

Your Fantastic Life is lived moment by moment. It's not a destination. So, if a win doesn't feel like a win anymore, listen to your psyche. When my love of running and that feeling of accomplishment it gave me started to wane, I simply moved to long hikes with my buddies Brad and Paul. Many of them were off-trail adventures in remote parts of the country. Those twenty, thirty, fifty, hundred-mile hikes were filled with wins, new wins, exciting wins that truly felt and still feel like wins to this day.

Our days hiking off trail, we never really know what we might face around the next bend, even with topographic maps in hand. The map is never the terrain. So just making it to the top of a peak, finding our way through a canyon, or wading across a river are huge wins. They feel great. But what if you are not on the trail getting those kinds of wins? I still want you to have wins in your day. I still want you to feel that dopamine rush of accomplishment. What do you do?

Well, I can't be on the trail every single day getting those kinds of highs. So here's what I do. Lately, I just walk right into my own closet. That's where I get my first win of the day and a whole bunch more. My wins are push-ups. First thing out of bed, I get down on the floor in my closet and do what started as one push-up. Throwing the covers off, getting up, and walking to my closet to do that one push-up was a way for me to get a win first thing and start my day in a winning mindset. I also got a win when that one push-up became a habit. I got another win when, after a few months, I added a second push-up. Everyone can get this kind of win first thing in the morning, right? It takes all of thirty seconds.

Remember back to Rule #4 Play Where You Can Win? This is an example of that too. If I had gotten out of bed and said, "I'm going to go to the gym and do fifty push-ups," fitting that in with the other things that are important to me wouldn't have worked. I wouldn't have gotten the win and all the good that comes with it. Instead, I played where I could win—in my closet—with a much more attainable goal: one tiny push-up. I'm sure you know where this goes. Today, hundreds of mornings into my push-up routine, I'm doing fifty push-ups and several other exercises too.

Here's another example. A few years ago, I started reading two pages from a book at the end of my pushups. Now I get my reading in every day. Win, win, win, win... . The whole routine takes me twenty minutes or less, no driving, no hassle, no reason to blow it off, and I rack up a ton of wins to start my day. This little game sets my mind, so I can both create and recognize more wins during my day. It's a surefire way to feel like a winner and be a winner, which makes for a Fantastic Life.

Recognize the Little Wins

Until you've trained your mind to go for and recognize the little things you do every day as wins, you may think these little achievements are simply, "meh!" Maybe it's calling your mother to say hello every morning or getting to the office 10 minutes early—no big deal, right? It's easy to minimize our accomplishments, isn't it? And if you're a person who has a habit of minimizing big accomplishments like scoring a promotion, finishing a triathlon, or closing a big client, then you most likely won't think making your bed in the morning is a win. But it is. Walking past someone and looking up from your phone, saying hello, smiling, and getting a hello back. That's a win.

You can get so many wins in a day, but until you start thinking, "get the win," you'll miss the opportunities that might lead to something you never expected and make for an even more Fantastic Life. How about if you're single and trying to meet that right partner? Wins include getting out of the house, joining a new club, and even letting friends know you accept referrals! Those can all be hard things to do, but when you stick your neck out, that's a win. Please recognize all the little things that are wins in your day. Go ahead and give them a fist bump.

> **Until you've trained your mind to go for and recognize the little things you do every day as wins, you may think these little achievements are simply, "meh!"**

Wins Start at the Bottom

In the previous chapter, you read about the humble beginnings and the early wins of Jeff Bezos, Richard Branson, Elon Musk, and my friend Mike Welborn. Their stories all had one thing in common: all four men achieved wins, many, many rungs down from where they are now. My first commercial real estate transaction—my first transaction win—was a 1,200-foot psychologist's office. From there, each deal—each win—got a little bigger and then, eventually, a lot bigger.

My wins weren't just signed lease transactions. Think about it; you can't close a transaction until you get a prospect. You can't get a prospect until you make some cold calls. And you can't make cold calls until you pick up the phone. Are you following me? The most important win that happened in my day back then is the same one that happens today. It's picking up the phone. Dial. Win!

Have you ever put off picking up the phone and connecting with a long-lost business colleague or friend? Certainly, they'd like to hear from you. And do you think that scoring that little win wouldn't lead to bigger wins? Do you think they might say, "Hey, since you called and now that I know what you're up to, I'm going to put you in touch with my friend." It happens, and bingo, another win! A warm lead! A new business opportunity! A new job lead! A potential partner! Imagine if you made a few calls every day. Not only would you rack up the wins, those actions would very likely transform your life.

Let Yourself Feel the Win

I love the quote by social scientist and author of Tiny Habits, B.J. Fogg. He says, "Give yourself 'shine' for that." What he means is, don't overlook your wins; give yourself credit. Let yourself shine a bit. **When you shine on the inside, you shine on the outside. Seeing your day, moment by moment, as a series of little wins turns you into a person other "win collectors" want to be around.** Those people are also called optimists and achievers, and they are sure more fun to be around than the negative pessimists who drag you down. To me, that's what makes you the kind of person people want in their circles. Even if your wins are small in the scheme of things, it doesn't matter. They're important to you, and they are making you shine, setting you up for even more wins.

Getting, recognizing, and celebrating wins regularly also helps you stay positive in the face of life situations that you know won't have a positive outcome. A friend and colleague who I admire so much shared the story of her father. Shortly after his eightieth birthday, he was diagnosed with terminal pancreatic cancer. Meet Danielle Feroleto.

"Literally the day after my dad's big surprise birthday party—almost a hundred people in the back yard—he said he wasn't feeling well. He said he

B.J. FOGG SAYS: "Give yourself 'shine' for that."

thought he ate too much cake. We laughed a little, but after his stomach pains didn't go away, he went to the doctor. Once they finally got to the bottom of what was going on, the news wasn't good. The doctors gave him four months to live. They told us, 'Go home and take care of him. I'm sorry, there's nothing we can do.'"

Recognize Wins are Everywhere

Danielle, a trained win collector, could have looked at this situation and thought there are no wins here, and there certainly wasn't going to be one in the end. It would have been completely understandable given the circumstances to see each day as a series of losses and just get through those last months of her father's decline, chalking it up to a very sad time in her life that easily could have been a crutch for the rest of her life. "Of course, we knew what the outcome was going to be and for me, just twenty-eight years old at the time, it was tough to think my dad wasn't going to see me get married, have kids, build a career or impact the world as an adult. I wasn't going to share being an adult with him and the guidance I so deeply valued. And I was going to miss him tremendously.

"But my sisters and I weren't going to let those precious days with our father be about our sadness. We were going to figure out how to be good caregivers and good supporters. When you know at the end that you're not going to get a win; instead, you're going to get defeat, you have to look for the wins, the blessings, in the midst of it all. In the moments. How could we make this time with our dad rich with wonderful memories, for him and for us, and that would outweigh the sadness we knew we were going to feel when he died? The way we did it was to find the blessings in the moment."

Among those blessings Danielle shared were little things that were really big things in retrospect. Like spending uninterrupted time together and learning things about her dad's life. "We found this little book with questions to ask your dad. We would lie on the bed with him and ask him about his life, and it was so fun hearing his stories from a simple question like 'What are your favorite foods?' That would trigger a bunch of memories for him about his childhood. Hearing that history was a win. The time my sisters and I got to spend with him was a win; normally, we're all so busy with our own lives. It brought us all closer than ever and developed an unbreakable bond that even supersedes natural sibling relationships. The compassion we witnessed from Hospice of the Valley was such a win. As a result, we shared a gift of my father's artwork that now hangs in the hallways of Hospice. Win. And I then eagerly started volunteering to be with patients as they experienced their last days of life. Another win.

"It was the sweetest journey we took with my dad. Ultimately, being right by his side as he took his last breath was a win that I would never have expected. Seeing his final days as a series of wins made all the difference.

Celebrate your successes— even small ones.

Honestly, that perspective wasn't a deliberate choice. Like, 'Let's find the wins in this awful situation.' It was more about recognizing one, then another, and another, realizing this process isn't all sadness. There are blessings here too. Then we did start looking for wins and, finally, finding ways to create them. It became a bit of a game."

Danielle lives her life with wins in mind. Relating to her business, she said, "We can look at a particularly difficult time—like the Great Recession, for example—and say, 'Oh, this is a horrible time.' Or we can say, 'You know these challenges we are facing, they create an opportunity for us to grow and strengthen our resilience that wouldn't have been there otherwise. If the Great Recession hadn't happened, we wouldn't be where we are now, which is on a much better path. Working smarter and as a more cohesive team.'" Danielle believes that as you grow teams and work on self-improvement, realize there will be challenges. "It's like working out and thinking, 'I used to be able to run ten miles. Now I can only run three.' That could be defeating, but you know what? I did the three, and it felt good. I did my workout today, and I made some progress. That's a win."

Not everything will go our way, but there is often incremental growth that you might not even see as happening in this moment. The situation is creating the opportunity, and your attitude is influencing it. You'll see this applies to Chapter 7, too which is all about Staying Out of The Gap.

Getting Wins Can and Will Define You

Danielle is saying that **you can make the worst of a situation, or you can make the best of it. But to put it in terms of a Fantastic Life, the best of it means getting wins.** "Looking back, those last months with my dad were a really meaningful time in my life. It shaped me into who I am. Today, even in my company, Small Giants, a full-service construction marketing agency for commercial real estate, I strive to get the win every single day. When the recession tanked the economy in 2008 and businesses were folding left and right, we never laid off anyone. We could have, but we didn't. Instead, we worked hard and got wins. I remember one day dancing around the office because we actually got a job and made $400. It wasn't much, but it was a win! That mindset defined our culture."

The wins through the COVID-19 pandemic were everywhere, too. "We got really tough and decided we're going to keep our track record and not lay anyone off. We have to make 'plan A' work because we planned for a win. We're not going to have a 'plan B' because that's not a win. We scored all kinds of wins like getting through the whole thing together and emerging at the other end a stronger team."

"Diamonds are made under pressure."

ORIGIN UNKNOWN

I think what you're seeing through Danielle is that **wins can and do happen everywhere. It's how you see the world.** When you can train your mind to get wins during the good times, imagine how much easier and more meaningful those wins will be during the challenging times. Danielle ended by sharing something someone once told her. "A friend told me, 'Diamonds are made under pressure.' That's exactly how I look at life. I know that when I get wins during those tough times, brilliance, like a diamond, will come from it. Getting wins, living that way, has changed my life." Fantastic, right?

Steps You Can Take

Start establishing a "Get A Win" mindset Begin by looking at yesterday, last week, or even an hour ago and see if you can recognize the small wins you might have achieved. Maybe it's the fact that you took a walk today. Maybe it's that you picked up your dry cleaning. Maybe you landed that big sale you were hoping for. Wins come in all sizes. What wins have you never considered wins?

Frame your winning day Think about your day in terms of wins and even play a game. "How can I get a win in the next hour?" Then the next one and the next, until your entire day is made up of wins you recognize. Practice doing this consistently for thirty days until you have internalized getting wins as a way of life.

5. Get a Win

Align your wins to your goals Once you're able to recognize the wins in your life, see how you can align them to your Fantastic Life goals. By doing that, you'll be able to see how each win moves you closer to achievement, but also makes the journey feel full of dopamine rushes that feel Fantastic.

Plan bigger wins As you get more skilled at nailing those smaller wins, start planning the bigger ones. If they seem too daunting or like they're just going to take too long, break the win down into a series of smaller wins you can achieve quicker. More dopamine means more Fantastic-ness!

Give yourself credit For some of us, that's a win by itself. Before you go to sleep at night, be mindful and grateful for the wins you accomplished in your day. How fortunate you are to be in a position to achieve and go for more the next day.

5. Get a Win

Thoughts

▎ Do you give yourself the time to celebrate the wins in your life? Why or why not?

▎ What benefits do you suppose would come from thinking in terms of wins in all areas of your life?

▎ How would thinking in terms of wins impact those around you?

▎ What can you do to remain mindful of wins until the mindset becomes a habit?

▎ How can you remember to look for wins all day long?

5 | Get a Win

the **FANTASTIC** LIFE revisited

"Discipline equals freedom."

- Jocko Willink

Fantastic Life Rule
Set Goals

Right off the top, let me say my entire Fantastic Life is spelled out. Everything. I think about everything I do. Everything I plan, what I execute or don't execute, is all based on goals. Lots of people think I'm a little crazy. It's usually people who don't have goals for themselves and let life just happen to them. It's people who live by the seat of their pants. They say, "Wow, Craig, you live a regimented life." To me, it's a little crazy *not* planning ahead, going through life, never knowing what you want, never creating and implementing a plan to get it, and never experiencing that Fantastic feeling of accomplishment. I don't understand these people. I believe Jocko Willink, who wrote a book called *Discipline Equals Freedom*, when he said, "Discipline equals freedom."

Goals are my personal road map. So, I can't imagine anyone going through life without having goals. I can't, because for me, how would I know my direction, how would I know what I'm working for, how would I know when I should push harder or give it up? How would I know what's next? One of the reasons why I'm so adamant today at my age about goals, as opposed to when I was younger, is because I've seen too many people get what they think they wanted in life. And then, with that accomplishment in hand, they find it wasn't what they wanted after all. And they're unhappy.

These people are not malcontents. They just never sat down during the process of living to figure out what life would be like working toward some undefined end and then accomplishing it. They didn't think about what their daily routine would be. How demanding it would be. If they knew the tradeoffs in advance, would that end still be important? Motivational? Or is it something they'd never want in a million years?

I see people set big rock goals all the time and never hit them. One hundred percent of the time, they're not very good at doing the work leading up to accomplishing the goal. I call that work *GRAVEL*, and it's the subject of my book *rocks GRAVEL sand*. In it, you learn methods for doing the hard work leading up to achieving a big rock goal. The book helps you know exactly what you're signing up for and if it's part of the Fantastic Life you want. Sometimes goals *sound better* than they actually are in real life.

A great example of what I've seen all too many times goes something like this: "I'm going to be a doctor."

"Why do I want to be a doctor?"

"Because it sounds good. You can make a lot of money. My mom wants me to be a doctor. And I think it would be cool to have people call me 'doctor.'"

Are those really good reasons to commit nearly a decade of your life and hundreds of thousands of dollars to schooling? Are you going to be happy tied to a medical practice and patients who may need you any time of the day? Is that the way you want your life to be? Ideally, you need to answer those questions before you embark upon what I call the sand work of medical school to achieve the big rock goal of being a doctor.

The process of answering those questions and more is called *GRAVEL*, and I have never read a goal-setting book —and I've read hundreds—that talked about what lies between a dream and the execution of the daily grind. Between the *rock* and the *sand*. One of the biggest tragedies is when you finally hit a goal you were certain you wanted, only to find you were wrong. You never thought about what it would mean to your life, and now you're stuck. To me, that scenario is just as bad, maybe worse, than not having any goals at all.

GRAVEL is the Key

Goal books will tell you to write your goals down. But it takes more than that to achieve them. **After you pull your goal list together, the next critical step is to be obsessed with the details *(GRAVEL)* about each *rock* goal you wrote down.** If you write down, "I want to be a doctor. I want to learn to fly a plane. I want to get my real estate license. I want to start eating healthier. I want to run a marathon." All that's good. But leave a whole bunch

ABRAHAM LINCOLN SAID:

"The best way to predict your future is to create it."

of room after every goal because underneath, you need to determine how exactly you're going to make any, or all of that, happen. What's it going to take to achieve this goal or that goal? How much money? How much time? What will I have to omit from my life to get one or more of these goals done? What other sacrifices am I going to have to make? Are there any other goals I'll have to put aside to achieve even one or two goals on my list? Thinking this way kind of changes things, doesn't it? The pie falls right out of the sky.

If after performing this goal-reality-check you're still excited about one of the goals, you may be on to one you really want to achieve. And continuing to go through the GRAVEL and the sand may be difficult but worthwhile to you if it means achieving this big rock goal that you determined is ultra-meaningful to the life you want to live. I hope you can see the difference between just "setting a goal" and "obsessing over the details" of a goal, in essence, doing the GRAVEL work continually toward a goal. Which one has the better chance of a happy ending? The one you wing? Or the one you thoughtfully work through to make a part of your being?

Setting goals and Rule #2, "Be Crystal Clear on What You Want," go hand in hand. When my hiking buddy, Brad, and I looked at what it would take for us to complete the Pacific Coast Trail hikes that we talked about in an earlier chapter, we weren't willing to do it anymore, even though hitting those 1,200 miles had been on my goal list for a decade. We thought about it and realized we didn't want to chase miles anymore. Same thing with being a pilot. I thought I wanted to do it, had it on my goal list, and knew exactly what I'd have to put aside to achieve that goal. This year, I cut it from my list. The tradeoffs weren't worth it. The goals I'm chasing, they mean a lot to me. And those two goals didn't.

People change. I changed, and therefore the goals that are important to us change sometimes too. I missed my window for the Pacific Coast Trail and for getting my pilot's license. But that's okay because I achieved other more meaningful goals. That's my point here. **Doing the GRAVEL work of discernment and planning is what makes goal setting and goal achieving both healthy and Fantastic.**

Goals Are Interconnected

Living the Fantastic Life is incorporating all your goals into one plan. As you do, you'll realize how **working on one goal impacts the goals in the other areas of your life.** The pieces shift all the time, so by having the goals that matter to you written down and organized so that you know exactly the path to achieving them, shifting them around isn't a problem. Here's what I mean. Let's say you have a goal to train for the Ironman race and eventually do whatever it will take to compete at the world championship in Kona, Hawaii. You also want to have children in the future, so you're working to be a good provider for your family's future. Your training schedule is seven

> People change. I changed, and therefore the goals that are important to us change sometimes too.

days a week, four hours a day, with longer bike rides and swims on the weekend. You work most nights and wake up to do the whole thing all over again.

One day, your wife tells you the good news. You both are expecting your first baby. It's a dream come true. Your goal of children is now becoming a reality. But let's be real, a newborn is going to impact your goal of getting to Kona. How could it not? So what do you do? Give up your goal? Forget Ironman? You're so close to qualifying. No, you go back to your goal sheet and look at your plan. What can you adjust to allow you to be a father and an Ironman triathlete? Without a plan and an understanding of how goals must adjust, you may have thought you were facing an either/or decision. Not so. Others have had kids and competed at Kona, so it can be done. I know it can be done. I ran the Western States 100, finished my MBA, was blessed with our first daughter, and was #1 at Lee & Associates, all in a fifteen-month period. Goal setting with *GRAVEL* works.

And that's the message of my dear friend and colleague, Charlie Dunlap. **Through a lifetime of accomplishments, one truth prevailed. "It's not can I do it? The question is, can it be done? If it can be done, then it's just a matter of figuring out how."** Charlie is so casual about all he has achieved, and much of it started by simply asking, "Can it be done?" That should lead us all to wonder what great things we could accomplish with that mindset.

Charlie's first goal, he remembers, was wanting to be class president in his Phoenix, Arizona, school. He won the election and learned early on that a first success begets a second one and a third one, and so on. Wins encourage more wins so long as you work hard and earn the respect of people around you. This was an excellent lesson to learn in 8th grade, and he carried it with him through college at the London School of Economics and into the army, where his goal was to get through the Vietnam War in one piece.

"I worked for the chief of intelligence, and it was my job to prepare a report on what the Vietcong were likely going to do next. Our intelligence group would gather up all the radio intercepts, interrogation reports, captured enemy documents, and information from well-paid spies. I would edit the material into a country-wide brief every two weeks. As dark as it was to learn the brutal tactics of the enemy, it was a window into what could be done, and mostly by young, impressionable kids. That was the enemy's method."

Post military, Charlie embarked on a career in real estate development. It was something he had never done before, but that was what intrigued him. He knew it could be done. Many apartment complexes had been built through history, so it wasn't new; it was just new to him. "What's the worst thing that could happen? You make a mistake and learn something. **I have never been ruled by fear. Instead, I have always had faith that I'd find the path. So taking risks was second nature as long as I knew it could be done.**" That's a philosophy Charlie has lived by his whole life.

CHARLIE DUNLAP SAYS:
"What's the worst thing that could happen? You make a mistake and learn something."

Goals Require Fearlessness

Charlie says the way to be secure in life is to not worry about being secure, to keep moving, and to never fear what's around the bend. "I used to hike a lot with friends, and whenever I had to stop to tie my shoelace—what seemed like just a few seconds—I would look up and be amazed at how far ahead the others on the hike would be by the time I pulled that shoelace tight. That's life. If you stop on your journey, the world keeps going. It's so much more fun to keep going with the wonderment of what's going to happen next. The path to your goal is fluid."

Change is inevitable. New jobs, marriage, divorce, children, grandkids, relocations... all of these things move the pieces of your goals around. They are all interconnected, and as long as your goals are meaningful to you and you have a solid understanding of what it will take to achieve them, you can make the necessary shifts. Personally, I'm doing more exercising than I have in a while because I'm training for a hike in Spain. Yes, I've had to remain dedicated but flexible, even when others around me are kicking back, like during a family vacation we took in Mexico.

Here's the dedication and flexibility part. My training schedule included a daily hike for a minimum of three hours with a 40-pound rucksack on my back. But being on vacation with all of us together, I didn't want to miss spending time with my family. So my adjustment to the change of venue and priorities was to wake up two hours before anyone else, before sunrise, and get my hike in. Some of my kids couldn't believe I'd do that on vacation. But I told them, "The trek I'm taking in Spain means a lot to me. I want to be able to do it." When you have a goal that really matters, you don't shirk your responsibilities because you don't want to shirk them.

My goals drive all my decisions. They are how I evaluate what I'm going to spend my time doing. They allow me to say "No" to things that aren't important. Sometimes that means saying "No" to myself. Especially when I want to be lazy. And we all want to be lazy sometimes. This is one of the secrets to getting a lot done and accomplishing a lot in life. This depth of goal setting keeps you disciplined, motivated, and moving forward.

Qualities of a Good Goal

Goals are also second nature to me. I can define a goal as easily as writing my name. But that's me. If goals are new to you, here are some quick guidelines for writing a goal that has the best chance of being accomplished:

Let's say your goal is to launch your new legal consulting business by January 1 and earn $100k by December 31.

The path to your goal is fluid.

Why is this goal achievable?

- » **It's specific** There's no question about what this goal aims to achieve.
- » **It's measurable** This goal includes a targeted annual income that is motivating.
- » **It's got a deadline** This will happen by the end of the year.
- » **It's in writing** This helps make it visible, memorable, and real.

This is the first step—a big *rock* goal. If there is one takeaway from this chapter (other than the importance of goal setting), it's to *do the GRAVEL work!* Take the time (and it is a lot of time) to really obsess over the goal details. Gather all the pieces, parts, and obstacles, and start them.

Steps You Can Take

It's time to write your goals. I'm sure while reading this chapter, some goals may have come to mind. Remember, as you think about your goals, try your best to envision what life would be like when you achieve them. Are those goals still appealing? Do any fall off the list once you really think them through? When you set your next goal, try writing it with these guidelines in mind:

Determine your goal's result Make sure you have a real motivating result as a part of your goal. Instead of "I want to lose weight," how about "I want to fit into my favorite jeans again by losing 15 pounds." Or instead of, "I'd like to explore Europe," say, "I want to go to Italy and hike Cinque Terre."

6 Set Goals

Set a target date Make sure the result has a defined end. "I want to fit into my favorite jeans again before my ten-year class reunion by losing 15 pounds." Or "I want to hike Cinque Terre July 8-12th."

Map out your steps List your steps for achieving the goal. You'll want to read my book rocks *GRAVEL* sand if you haven't already. It will show you how to really plan out the steps. Be sure to break your goal down into little achievable pieces, so you get regular wins. That's a start. So for that first goal example, if you're aiming to lose weight, the *GRAVEL* might look like this:

» Step 1: Assess my current food intake and write it down.

» Step 2: Eliminate one unhealthy choice per week and add in one healthy choice per week.

» Step 3: Assess my current weekly schedule and find 30 minutes per day for exercise.

You get the idea...obsess. Otherwise, it won't happen. And if it does happen, you won't be ready.

List your obstacles What are the things that will derail your plans? Things like your work schedule, your kid's extracurricular activities, the junk food in your pantry, etc. Know them in advance.

Set Goals

Set a strategy for each obstacle Since you know the pitfalls, make a plan for how you'll avoid them. For example, I'll set my alarm an hour earlier than normal. I'll delegate kid taxi service to my partner two days a week. I'll stop buying junk food at the grocery store, etc.

Take daily action No matter how small, get a win every day toward your goal.

Review your progress weekly and monthly If you've kept at it, this should be a fun part of the process. You have to check in regularly and adjust as needed.

6 Set Goals

Thoughts

▪ Do you have worthy goals in all the important areas of your life?

▪ What are you going to have to sacrifice to achieve your goals?

▪ Are you still crystal clear on what you want now that you know what it will take; is it still worth it to you?

▪ What, if anything, would you change?

▪ *GRAVEL* is obsession. *GRAVEL* is mandatory. Accept that.

6 Set Goals

the **FANTASTIC** LIFE® revisited

The Gap is that space between where you are and your notion of that ideal place you feel you should be.

Fantastic Life Rule

Get Out of The Gap

The Gap is a concept I learned from being part of the Strategic Coach® program. So powerful is this idea, I made it one of my Fantastic Life Rules decades ago. If you want to dive deeper into The Gap and The Gain™ concept created by Dan Sullivan, I strongly suggest you read the best-selling book The Gap and The Gain by Dan Sullivan and Ben Hardy. To me, it is a must-read for a Fantastic Life.

The reason I say all this at the start of this chapter is because no matter what you do in life, whether you're single, married, employed as an executive, salesperson, teacher, doctor, carpenter, or rocket scientist, you wander into and out of The Gap all day long. Those of us living a Fantastic Life have learned how to get ourselves out as quickly as possible when we fall into The Gap (and we do all the time).

The Gap is that space between where you are and your notion of that ideal place you feel you should be. Here are a few examples.

The Gap in the workplace *"I'm a VP, and I'm 45 years old. I really should be farther ahead by now. I used to want to start my own business. What the hell?"*

The Gap in a family "I'm always disappointed by our family's holiday get-togethers. I just want them to be like they were when we were all kids, and they never are. Kind of sucks."

The Gap with kids "I always thought my son would want to play baseball like I did. I always saw him going to a Division 1 school on scholarship and maybe even playing professionally. It didn't work out that way."

The Gap with love "Where are all the good men? I don't believe in fairy tales, but I do expect there to be at least a few Prince Charmings out there who appreciate a strong, confident female. So far, I've kissed a bunch of frogs who stayed frogs. A few became toads."

Life in The Gap is anything but Fantastic. In fact, it's pretty depressing to always look at what you *haven't* achieved in life rather than what you have. Dan Sullivan defines The Gap as that place between where you *are* and where you *think* you should be, and **if you let your mind stay in The Gap for any length of time, well, let's just say life can really suck.**

Life feels very different when you measure yourself against your ideals versus measuring yourself against your own *progress* toward your goals. **When you measure yourself and your idea of happiness or accomplishment or completeness or success against some notion of perfection that is never attainable, you are living in The Gap.** And if we are goal setters, we are bound to fall into The Gap numerous times a day. The key is to quickly recognize when you are there and learn how to get out of it.

How to Get Out of The Gap

We live in a very connected world, and it is easy to let society place us in constant comparison with others. It is all too easy to get stuck measuring your life next to other people's lives, or at least the lives they portray through social media. Talk about a recipe for falling into The Gap! If social media wasn't bad enough, the worst of it is the ready comparisons between your life and everyone else's. **Here's the first important method for getting out of The Gap: Judge where you are based on your own goals and progress toward those goals, not to the appearances or ideals of others.**

I've always been ultra-competitive, but at this point in my life, I seldom find myself in head-to-head competition. Sure, at Lee & Associates, where I work, we have sales contests, rankings, and awards for the top sales teams, and we always go for the top spot. We have won a lot, and maybe it's because we don't compete directly with the other sales teams. Instead, we set our goals, work them, and then continually find ways to self-improve. We're always striving to get better and do more every single day. If another team posts a big deal that puts them ahead, we feel the competitive juices flow. Quickly, we pull ourselves out of The Gap by self-directing

Why fret The Gap? Instead, say, "Hey, there's The Gap. What is the learning? What is my next step? What motivation can I take from this experience? Where will this take me?" As Dan Sullivan says, "Where is the Gain?"

our own tasks and getting busy. We use the other team's success as motivation. It's never a comparison of us versus them.

Remember Danielle Feroleto from Rule #5 - Get a Win? She manages to get out of The Gap by not judging herself or her company based on others or where they are at that moment. Instead, she looks for the wins. Sometimes they take the shape of a current hardship that is bringing the team closer together. Sometimes it's self-improvement. She is the master of recognizing The Gap as a gift, and as the required motivation to achieve her goal.

You'll find, once you start looking at life this way, that **there are infinite sources of motivation for creating goals and staying on course to achieve them.** You may not reach the ideal, but you'll get a lot closer than you would have otherwise. This is where personal and professional growth takes place and isn't that the lasting benefit? Why fret The Gap? Instead, say, "Hey, there's The Gap. What is the learning? What is my next step? What motivation can I take from this experience? Where will this take me?" As Dan Sullivan says, "Where is the Gain?"

The philosopher Seneca said what's required is **"Confidence in yourself and the belief that you are on the right path, and not led astray by the many tracks which cross yours of people who are hopelessly lost."** And isn't that exactly what happens? People who are far less confident, far less accomplished, far less directed—Facebook and Instagram are both full of them—and who barely know you weigh in. Why let them influence you on what you should do next? Worst of all, in those lower moments, be honest, do you compare yourself to them and the "Fantastic Life" they seem to be living? Maybe their life is fantastic, but in most cases, it is not. Which leads me to why I wrote this book in the first place. To help people live an authentically Fantastic life.

Another Way to Get Out of The Gap

It feels like human nature to measure ourselves against our ideals, which by definition, are unreachable. When we do that, we are constantly unhappy or hurt or disappointed. But what if you use your ideals to direct you, to give you guidance and motivation? You can choose your point of reference. "Look how far I have come. I would never have believed it a year ago! Look how much I have learned. How much I have grown." **Always measure backward. Always measure your growth. That's the second key to getting out of The Gap.**

All you do is take whatever experience you might have had and reframe it. Mark this page and re-read Rule #1 – Know Your Stories. Here's a story: Let's say you got married when you were twenty-eight and thought it would last forever. Then twenty-five years later, you find yourself divorced and wondering how you ended

HENRY FORD SAID:
"When everything seems to be going against you, remember that the airplane takes off against the wind, not with it."

up alone at age fifty-three. That wasn't the plan. Right there, that experience of a failed marriage could quickly become The Gap. "I'm so not where I planned to be at this age. I didn't expect to be alone. This is far from my ideal life."

Sadly, that's how many people would frame a situation like that. And it's understandable to a point. But the sooner you move past The Gap by reframing the experience, the better. Rather than lament where you are or the time spent in a doomed marriage, look to what you accomplished instead. Maybe it is a better understanding of yourself, human nature, or what you truly want in life and what you don't. Perhaps it's recognizing you're closer to living a Fantastic Life now than you would be by avoiding the truth about your marriage. Know your stories!

It's all how you frame and measure where you are in your life at this very moment. Are you viewing that place as one where you are falling short? Or are you viewing it as truth, growth, and progress? You need to make that choice to get out of The Gap.

A master of this technique is my friend and business partner, Dean Bloxom. Dean is a pioneer in the retail mortgage lending space, having founded a company called imortgage that LoanDepot eventually acquired. He also recognizes the importance of reframing the difficult times he's experienced and credits this mindset for getting out of The Gap faster. **Dean says that when you look back at your life, there are always dark and difficult times that could cause despair, sadness, and failure. "The thing is, you're going to get out of it. When you look**

backward, you always do, so why not this time? Everybody gets out of it, that is, people who want to be relatively successful, people like us, we always get through it. And so, in the middle of difficult times, I've always said to myself, 'Well, I'm going to get through this, and when I do, this will be all in the past. And after, I know I'll feel thrilled to be beyond it.' So I start putting myself into that feeling before I get there, and guess what? I get there a lot faster."

Although Dean cautions trying to set a timeframe for when you'll feel better and emerge from The Gap, he does tell people they will feel better in the future. The sooner you can begin to imagine what the future will feel like and actually feel it even a little, the sooner you will move beyond the hardship. "I spend a lot of time looking at what that end result will be. And I put myself there. Like we're going to double the size of our company every year for the next five years. I imagine very vividly what that is going to look like. And then—this is where it gets really scary for most people—I start talking about it a whole lot. Like it's already happened. And that puts everybody in the same boat. I talk about it with confidence that it is 100% going to happen. I tell everyone this is what it will feel like when we get there. And this is why we're doing what we're doing. I want everyone to see what that vision looks like and feels like. I tell anybody and everybody who will listen because **here's a truth: The more often you talk about something, the more likely it is to happen.**"

> The sooner you can begin to imagine what the future will feel like and actually feel it even a little, the sooner you will move beyond the hardship.

7 Get Out of The Gap

Along the path, there are going to be ups and many downs. Dean says to keep focused on how it feels to achieve your vision and constantly measure where you are in terms of your progress. If you stall, instead of wallowing, take action and make small adjustments. Pivot from inaction to action. Again, reframe the situation and, like Danielle in Chapter 5, celebrate the wins.

How Do You Know You're in The Gap?

Dean is a perfect example of a leader who knows The Gap will happen and sets himself up with a system of visualization and action for getting out of it. It's brilliant! Dan Sullivan coaches the idea that **The Gap is a place of scarcity and fear. It's a place of zero appreciation for where you are and how far you've come. It's a place of feeling a sense of loss, sadness, and unworthiness. So, if you feel any of that, you're in The Gap.** I know, none of this sounds like a Fantastic Life, which is why you must get out of The Gap as quickly as possible. There's no burying it. All of us get into The Gap. And we do it all the time. The secret is to recognize and get out of The Gap. I find that simply by knowing the concept, I can get out of The Gap pretty fast. Being aware of The Gap, expecting it, and knowing the signs does wonders for getting out of it quickly.

Seneca's wisdom confirms what we're talking about here too. He said, **"It is better to conquer our grief than to deceive it. For if it has withdrawn, being merely beguiled by pleasures and preoccupations, it** starts up again and, from its very respite, gains force to savage us. But the grief that has been conquered by reason is calmed forever." He is saying, don't deny that you're in The Gap. Recognize it and get out of it not through distractions but by reasoning. In my world, that means looking for The Gain. In Danielle's world, it means recognizing the win. And in Dean's world, it means having a vivid vision of what getting out of The Gap looks and feels like and then feeling it before it happens.

How often do people go for the "beguiled pleasures and preoccupations," as Seneca put it? Alcohol, drugs, food, TV, video games, social media, sleeping, anything that takes the pain away. We've all been there. None of us is perfect. But you and I both know what happens next. You wake up the next day, and the pain is still there. That's why **you have to reframe the moment and think of it as a valuable experience on the path to your goal and get out of The Gap as fast as you can before it becomes a trap.**

I can go into The Gap about the fact that I've lost my hair! It sounds trivial, but it's real. I can fall into The Gap because of my inevitable aging. When that happens, I reframe my "Gap moment" by thinking instead that my lack of hair symbolizes my wisdom, accomplishment, and continued growth. It's a reminder that I am happy to be alive as a cancer survivor. And that at my age, there

> **Being aware of The Gap, expecting it, and knowing the signs does wonders for getting out of it quickly.**

aren't many things I can't do. Those are all wins to savor while remaining hopeful that modern medicine comes up with an easy and effective hair restorer!

The Gap is Inevitable

No matter what area of your life we're talking about, falling into The Gap is going to happen. Even with seemingly little things like burning the chocolate chip cookies you're baking or eating too many of the chocolate chip cookies you baked. How fast can you get out of it and recover that feeling of Fantastic? Well, now you know the concept and the solution. Look for The Gain. The Gap has a way of throwing us off kilter. It can make us emotional, and when that happens, rational thinking goes out the window. You know The Gap will happen, so start shaping the pattern of your Fantastic Life responses to it now. Be mindful before you run into The Gap because you won't be when The Gap happens. The sooner you begin shaping this habit, the more Fantastic your life will be.

Steps You Can Take

Take inventory When have you fallen into The Gap in the past? Is it in your work life, your personal life, or your health? All of them? The idea here is to see if there are any patterns. It is all too easy to use one aspect of your life to avoid the shortcomings you feel in another area of your life. That avoidance isn't a solution. Instead, recognize The Gap and use the techniques in this chapter to get out and stay out.

7
Get Out of The Gap

Prepare for other "Gap Moments" You know the Gaps will happen, so rather than hide from the inevitable, decide in advance The Gain you'll put in motion to get out of them. If social media always makes you feel like a failure, then plan to do something else when you get the urge to peruse Facebook or Instagram. Instead, call a friend, or write in your journal about your wins and progress toward your goal. Have a plan for what you'll do to get out of The Gap before it happens.

Record your feelings When The Gap happens, write down how you feel and what your response is. Sometimes that exercise alone is very clearing. Just wallowing gets you nowhere. But when you write down your feelings and force yourself to think and write your actions, you are back in the driver's seat. In essence, you are reframing your stories.

Do a little assessment The next time you find yourself in The Gap, or maybe think about the last time, ask yourself, "How long did it take me to get out of The Gap?" As Dean Bloxom said, you are going to get out of it, so you may as well act as if you already are there. How long did it take to change your mindset and which method was the most effective for you? That way you'll know your best methods for the future.

7 | Get Out of The Gap

151

 Thoughts

- How often do you find yourself in The Gap?

- What are your triggers?

- Are you viewing your life against an ideal life instead of progress toward your goals?

- How can you reframe The Gap so that you recognize The Gain?

- What would your life look like and feel like if you could get out of The Gap faster?

7
Get Out of The Gap

the **FANTASTIC LIFE** revisited

The Fantastic Life is one where you achieve not one big rock goal, but a number of big *rock* goals. Which means, you are working on them all at the same time.

Fantastic Life Rule

Use the 2% Rule

The Fantastic Life is one where you achieve not one big rock goal but a number of big rock goals. Which means you are working on them all at the same time. And you're doing everything else you have to do in your life. Like taking care of kids, managing employees, taking your car in for an oil change, ordering stuff online, returning stuff you ordered online, and making sure your dog is fed and walked all before 10 am. Really? You're going to live your life and manage all your responsibilities, big and small, AND achieve big rock goals all at the same time. Impossible!

We've all heard the saying, give 100% in everything you do. Okay, that's good if it gets you past being a 50% performer. But what if you are someone who does give your all or close to it? Giving 100% day in and day out can be demotivating in my mind because it doesn't quantify what you're measuring. It just says, "Go for broke." What is 100% anyway? But when you do ten push-ups every day, and then you add one more, now that's quantifiable. And that accomplishment feels good.

Then there's this idea I'm sure you've heard. If you want to achieve anything, you have to give 110%. So if you want to achieve six goals—a family goal, professional goal, athletic goal, spiritual goal, personal goal, and community goal—you have to give 110% to every one of them. That's 660%, and that is not mathematically possible. I am pretty sure it is not humanly possible to keep that up for any extended period of time. That's how burnout happens and how goals fly out the window, unattained.

If anyone knows about overdoing it to simply achieve a goal, that person is me. Well, the former me. The lengths I used to go to, all in the name of getting to the finish line, were extreme, even by my standards. I used to think I needed to give 110% with everything. That's before I realized that overtaxing myself was not the most fantastic way to live my life. That was before I realized that instead of crushing it, I just had to give a little bit more, 2% more, every day, every week, every month, and every year. Just a little more.

My guess is you have never been taught the 2% Rule. My guess is that putting the pedal to the metal is what you always thought it takes to achieve any level of success. And that's how successful business people, athletes, performers, etc. do it. Furthermore, I'm pretty sure that the thought of doing that with all the pressures already staring you in the face, you might think, "Yeah, I'll take on that goal of starting a business maybe next year when I have more time." Or, "As soon as my youngest gets into elementary school, I'll have time to go to the gym every day and lose these extra pounds."

Here's the thing. **You never have the time to do everything. But you probably do have 2%'s worth of time right now. And even 2%'s worth of motivation.** That doesn't sound that hard, does it? In fact, you can put this book down right now and do just a little bit of something you've been meaning to do. Like if you want to get into a sit-ups routine, get on the floor and do two right now. Not 200 sit-ups. Just two. And then tomorrow, do three.

Ask Yourself This Question

How can I do a little bit more today? That's the question. Ask yourself that consistently, and you will change your life. How can I do a little bit more today toward my job search? How can I do a little bit more today to eat healthier? How can I do a little bit more today to double my income in two years? How can I do a little bit more today to show my family how much I love them?

Then when you answer those questions with a 2% Rule answer that is just a little more, before you know it, you're working toward and achieving a bunch of goals and living a Fantastic Life in the process.

Let's say, for example, you already do 2% more than your peers because you make a point of sending thank you notes to people who do something nice for you. Many people

> How can I do a little bit more today? That's the question. Ask yourself that consistently, and you will change your life.

send an email or a text thank you, but you've got this. You send hand-written thank you notes. And you mail them with a stamp—really nice touch. You already have a great habit that sets you apart. You can stick with that, but why not ask yourself, "What else can I do?"

I asked myself that exact question a while back. I already was in the habit of sending thank you notes, so when I asked myself, "How can I do a little more?" The answer that came back to me was, "Craig, send notes for reasons other than saying thank you. Send notes for no reason, just to let people know how much you value them, how important they are in your life." So, I started writing notes for no defined reason.

This practice has helped strengthen many relationships and has been the foundation for forging new ones. But that's not why I decided this activity would be my 2% for this habit; it was truly because life's short, and why not let people know they are awesome while you can? But here's the unexpected, Fantastic part that always comes from the 2% Rule in one way or another: This little effort of writing notes is helping me see and affirm just how Fantastic my life really is. How grateful I am for all these people in my life. Had I not committed to doing a little more, just 2% more, I would have completely missed receiving this gift.

Now, I know you have many Fantastic people in your life. Writing notes to the Fantastic people in my life is one of my 2% Rule efforts. What if it became yours, too? Would it change how you see the people around you? Maybe cause you to reflect upon who you have in your life—good, bad, or indifferent. Are they helping you get to where you want to go? Are you helping them? You can see how **the 2% Rule is so much more than just doing "a little more" and adding to your to-do list. It is an opportunity to take you from your everyday life into a new reality.**

The Important Second Part

Now that you know that the first secret for using the 2% Rule is simply to ask this question throughout the day, "How can I do a little bit more today?" When you answer that question, you are setting yourself up for some natural awakenings. Here's the second secret: How can I do a little bit more **every day**? Yes, on a daily basis, as a habit, for decades. That's how Fantastic changes and Fantastic growth happen. Consistency is the magic.

The real magic of the 2% Rule is that making those little deposits eventually creates a tidal wave of Fantastic. It's no different from the magic of compound interest and how much money you end up with when your savings grow over time. The compounding effect of exercising works the same way. Save or work out every so often, and you get nothing out of it. Save something every week or build upon your workouts daily—one dollar, one push-up,

MICHAEL PHELPS SAYS:
"If you want to be the best, you have to do the things other people aren't willing to do."

then two, then three, and magic happens. And it's gratifying to rack up those daily wins, ultimately achieving more than you ever thought possible.

I can't think of one instance where being consistent hasn't paid off for me in some way, and it will happen for you too. It happens when you save money, exercise, and work. It also happens when you consistently show love to your kids, partner, and friends. How about respect? When you consistently show respect to people around you. When you consistently take responsibility. When you consistently celebrate accomplishments and others' achievements. Nothing but good in my life has come from being consistent.

And how can you expect to really shine when the pressure is on if you haven't done a little bit extra every day? The fact is you won't shine, or at least not to the peak of your current ability. **You have to practice stretching your limits, and when you do 2% more every day, you build on what you did the day before. You're constantly creating a new baseline for what 100% looks like.**

Here are some simple examples of the 2% Rule to give you ideas of how easy powerful this rule can be:

» Not a reader?
Read 1-2 pages a day.

» Don't exercise? *Do one push-up.*

» Want a better relationship?
Call that person now just to say hi.

» Want to learn a new language?
Spend 3 minutes listening to it.

» Need more sales?
When you are done calling, make one more call.

Now, do all these again tomorrow and add a little bit more. And the next day, and the next. "Don't break the chain," as Jerry Seinfeld says.*

> *Jerry Seinfeld has a famous method for becoming a better comic. He said the way to create better jokes was to write every day. After a few days, you'll have a chain. Just keep at it, and the chain will grow longer every day. You'll like seeing that chain, especially when you get a few weeks under your belt. Your only job is not to break the chain.*

GRANT CARDONE SAYS: "Go the extra mile; there's no one on it."

2% Often is Doing for Others

Why do so many people love this Fantastic Life rule? Why does it mean so much in their lives? The 2% Rule is golden for so many people I know, and Curt Johnson, my friend and business associate, is no exception. The former president of First American Title, Curt has a lifetime of stories demonstrating the power of the 2% Rule. When I asked him about it, he was quick to say that yes, he always went that extra mile; he was the one who made sure he got those last emails out before getting in the car to drive home, usually with his headlights on. He absolutely did 2% more than others around him, and that effort, over time, catapulted him to a top post in a Fortune 500 international company.

"Those Saturday or Sunday cross-country flights to be ready for a breakfast meeting in New York or Washington first thing Monday morning were sacrifices. But I made those sacrifices because they helped my family, myself, and were for the good of the company."

But learn a little more about Curt, and you'll see what he considers the real key to his Fantastic Life. Beyond pulling long hours, making sacrifices, and as he puts it, "sheer luck and winning the Super Lotto" when it comes to his family, the "golden" 2% Rule for Curt is inseparable from The Golden Rule itself: "Do unto others as you would have others do unto you."

"I picked my mom and dad very carefully," Curt said jokingly. "They taught me to treat people not just how I wanted to be treated, but a little better than that." You might say 2% better! "So much of my happiness and whatever success I've had professionally has happened because I followed that rule. So when everyone else called it quits or made a habit of doing just enough to get by, I never did either of those things. Sure, success is about hustle, but for me, it has always been about doing things the right way for other people."

Curt makes all too clear that the 2% Rule involves more than simply working harder. It's caring about the people around you, above and beyond what's considered business as usual. "My dad moved us to Arizona with his job in retail in 1956. He went on to develop many of the major shopping malls in the Phoenix metro area during the decades that followed. They were game-changer projects for the local economy at that time.

"I watched him practice the 2% Rule as a young kid when I walked into the stores he helped build. He was a humble, quiet guy, but we'd walk into those department stores like Goldwaters and Diamonds, and he knew everyone. He'd greet them, ask about their lives and truly care when he heard their replies.

"They never forgot him for that, and the impression it made on me shaped my life too. For my

> ...the 2% Rule involves more than simply working harder. It's caring about the people around you, above and beyond what's considered business as usual.

dad, 2% meant taking that extra time to get to know someone and then giving 2% more day in and day out to stay connected with them. My dad naturally worked that way; however, I'm sure there were plenty of times when he had to make a choice between listening to someone's problems or calling it a day and heading home to his family. Looking back, I learned how much can collectively get done when you take time to get to know people."

2% Takes on Many Forms

The 2% Rule comes in many forms, as you can see: Doing the work, putting the time in, and caring about others is one way. For Maria Luna, the founder and CEO of Famigo, a startup platform for artists and creators, the relationship between the 2% Rule and doing for others started early in her life.

"I grew up in Puerto Rico. My mother was a widow, and she supported six of us, all living under one roof. As a little child, I saw her working and doing her best to provide for us. To describe the level of poverty we experienced in the 1970's at the time, is beyond words. She was making $1 an hour, which was well below the poverty line. Everything she did was out of love for us, so maybe that's why I always saw her instinctively do more, more, more. She used to ask us to do more in everything we did too. She would recite this quote from the Catholic faith: 'Do ordinary things in extraordinary ways.'

"Growing up, we were all required to use the meager resources we had in extraordinary ways. If that resource was time, money, food, whatever

came to us, use it for good, for progress. Don't ever squander it. Applying that rule became and is instinctive to me. It's the 2% Rule and to me, doing the most good with what you have is what life is all about.

"I remember asking one of my teachers, 'How do I stop being poor?' She told me you have to study hard and you have to work hard. So whenever I was preparing for an exam or doing homework, I always did extra. Like solving a few more geometry problems than required. Through that, I was able to think faster during the exams. I didn't have to do 10 or 20 more problems, just one or two with each assignment. Amazing how that works. Today I do the same with exercise. For example, I can hold plank position for over two minutes now. How'd I get there? By starting with 15 seconds and adding a second or two each time."

Maria's company continues to grow, taking the services it provides its user base of artists, musicians, comedians, small business owners, and more to new levels by continually adding more services like direct messaging fans, allowing content creation, and more. She is always looking for ways to use the resources she has to their fullest to grow the company. She says 2% is less about comparing herself *to* others and more about improvement *for* others. "And through that, I keep growing and getting better and better."

...doing the most good with what you have is what life is all about.

Living a Fantastic Life is by no means a passive life. But it does not have to be a daunting one either. In fact, it's the opposite. It's a life of doing a little more every day and feeling really good about it. You don't have to be perfect. Every day doesn't have to be perfect (and it won't be). But each morning, when you wake up, you have another chance to do 2% more throughout the day. Take it. Make it a part of who you are.

Steps You Can Take

Take another look at your goals Return to the goals you wrote down and review why you are doing them and who reaps the benefits. As Maria said, the 2% Rule is not about comparing yourself to others but doing for others. What part of your goals benefits others around you? What part of your goals benefits you? Which ones do both?

Do an effort assessment Ask yourself and assign a value to how much effort you are currently putting into each of your goals. It can be a number from one to ten, or it can be even simpler than that. I use a color code system: Green means I'm putting in a lot of effort, Yellow is some effort, and Red is little to no effort. Are you okay with that assessment?

8 Use the 2% Rule

Decide your 2% more for each Write down what giving just 2% more would look like for each of your goals. After your assessment, you may feel bad that those goals in red aren't getting more attention. Don't worry; this is your time to be aware and add 2% more effort. One thing, however, is to avoid the temptation to write down more than 2% on those goals you marked in Red. This isn't about playing catch up; it's about giving a sustainable 2% more consistently. Do more than that, and you likely will not be willing or able to keep up the pace.

Do a little time management Once you know your 2% for each of your goals, figure out how you will fit the extra effort into your day, keeping it really simple, like, "I'll just take a 10-minute shower instead of 15, so I can do my ten ab crunches." You'll find that miraculously, you have the time.

Make your 2% visible Write down your daily 2% for each goal on your goal spreadsheet, in your calendar app, on a sticky note, whatever works for you. Keep it simple, like "+1 crunch/day." Then put it somewhere you can see it. After about 30 days, you won't need the reminder because your 2% will become a habit. You'll need a new 2%.

8. Use the 2% Rule

Celebrate your wins ▍ Consistently doing 2% more is a win, so be sure to give yourself accolades for your achievements. If you've fallen short, don't beat yourself up. Just commit to getting back on track tomorrow. It's a great feeling to know your life is filled with positive effort, energy, and outcomes.

Make 2% a part of who you are ▍ The first step is to do the GRAVEL work so whatever you decide to do is meaningful, actionable, and sustainable. The second part is simple. Whatever you do today – add a little more. Just 2% more. Make everything you touch a little better. Then grow this into a habit and, ultimately who you become.

171
Use the 2% Rule

Thoughts

▌ What are some ideas for doing 2% more in your life that might stretch you but that would deliver results? There are always many options.

▌ What is keeping you from moving toward your goals? Why are you in the Green zone with one goal and in the Yellow or Red with others?

▌ Are the goals in the Yellow or Red zones still important to you?

▌ How did you feel when you excelled at achieving a goal? Did you feel great? Why or why not?

▌ How can you hold yourself to 2% every day? What system will work for you?

▌ What's something you can do this very minute that is 2% more?

173

Use the 2% Rule

the **FANTASTIC** LIFE revisited

Without pain
there is no
growth.

Fantastic Life Rule

Recognize There are Two Kinds of Pain

Pain happens. It just does, even while living your Fantastic Life. **A Fantastic Life does not mean a pain-free life, but it does mean you can choose the kind of pain you let into your life.** Choose your pain? How about no pain? Nice try, but as the famous saying goes, "No pain, no gain!" You know that truth. Without pain, there is no growth. Getting out of your comfortable state is what it takes to experience new things, overcome obstacles, and live life more prepared for the next challenge you face. If you haven't yet experienced the Fantastic feeling that comes from doing the hard thing, the thing you thought was beyond you, I hope this book leads you to do it.

What kind of pain do you currently have in your life? Everyone has some, physical or emotional. Maybe you have back pain. Or perhaps you struggle with the loss of an important relationship like a spouse or partner. Is your pain the sad fact that you and your kid just don't get along, and that really hurts? Maybe you travel a lot and feel bad about missing your kid's basketball games. Or how about the nagging guilt that if you would just *start* exercising, that back pain would probably go away?

Earlier in this book, you learned about setting goals, getting wins, and staying out of The Gap. What do all those rules have in common? Well, built into all of them is pain, which, I admit, doesn't sound very fantastic. **Let's be clear; you are going to experience pain achieving your goals, getting those little daily wins, and getting out of The Gap. But which kind of pain? Again, the choice is yours.**

The First Kind of Pain

Let's say you've been studying for the LSAT exam for months. You've locked yourself away from family, given up time with friends, missed playing golf, blew off parties, and basically lived a hermit's life because the score you get on this exam will mean the difference between getting into Harvard Law School or not. Harvard is your goal, and you believe you need a near-perfect score even to be considered.

Have the last six months been painful? Yes absolutely. Getting up at 4:00 am to study for two hours, getting your workout done, showering and heading to work, studying during lunch, working until 6:00 pm, then getting back on the study grind from 8:00 in the evening until you finally shut it down at 1:00 am. Every night and on weekends, it's more of the same except that your "work" is studying.

Half your friends think you're crazy and the other half admire your dedication. Both secretly wish they had your focus. You make it look easy, but is it? Hell, no! It sucks! It's painful! And it gets old missing out on the fun everyone else is having. But you press on with that in-your-face Harvard crest screensaver floating around on your computer, the Post-It note on your bathroom mirror you purposely see every day that simply says, "Goal: Harvard Law." The Harvard Law sweatshirt your husband bought you, thinking you'd like it.

This little tale demonstrates the first kind of pain: The Pain of Discipline. It happens because **living a Fantastic Life means you can have anything you want. You just can't have everything. And that trade-off causes the Pain of Discipline.** This kind of pain is hard in the present moment. Sitting, focusing, and studying for a life-defining exam is hard. So is traveling three weeks out of the month, every month, because your career path demands it. So is running 100 miles a week to train for an ultra-marathon like the Marathon des Sables, a race we talked about earlier in this book. Achieving your Fantastic Life goals will take a ton of discipline. And that's why I say it will be painful... in the moment.

The Second Kind of Pain

Let's go back to your Harvard goal. Congratulations! You studied, and now, here it is, the week of the LSAT exam. You feel ready and just to double-check your planned arrival time, you look at your calendar and notice that the night before the exam is the biggest football game of the year, and you've been invited. All your old college friends are getting together at the local sports bar to relive their college years. It's a tradition to get together for this big rivalry.

"How can I miss this? I go every year. Ugh! I can't believe it's this weekend. I can't break tradition; I only get to see these people once a year," your inner voice goes back and forth and makes a pretty good case.

Your other inner voice chimes in with a pretty good argument, too, "You've studied so hard. What you'll need is a good night's sleep, so you can wake up fresh and be ready to go. Stay focused."

"That's just it. You have studied so hard. You deserve a little fun, blow off steam, and clear your head before the test. It will do you good," you say to yourself, half believing it really might do you some good.

"Are you out of your mind? A football beer bash? Risk your entire dream for a college football game! You're a fool," the back and forth continues. It continues until, at last, you reach a decision.

"You know what, I'm going to go for just a few hours. I won't drink any beer; just say hi to all my friends, blow off a little steam, leave at half-time, and all will be well."

Easier said than done when the game is tied, and it's beer and shots all around. If you can leave after one beer before the nail-biter game is over, that's the Pain of Discipline at play. But what if you don't leave? What if you get swept up in the moment, and that moment lasts until midnight? You make your way home and manage to set your alarm for 6:00 am. When it chimes, you feel like you were hit by a truck. "Oh shit, what have I done? How could I be so stupid?" You peel yourself out of bed, get dressed, and head out to take the exam. Your head is pounding, and you feel a little sick to your stomach. "Shit! What was I thinking?" Coffee doesn't even taste good.

You know where this story goes. You take the exam, and score well, considering, but not well enough. Harvard and your Fantastic Life goal will have to wait. You want to kick yourself because the game was fun, but not *that* fun. "We didn't even win." Certainly not fun enough to blow your chances at Harvard. "I'm a year behind now in making it to Harvard, at best! And for what? A party? Ugh!"

It takes weeks for you to let go of your anger and start exploring plan Bs and other law schools. And just when you think you're over it, you hear in your head, "Why? Why did I go to that damn party? If I could just relive that one night..." Ten years later, you're vying for partner at the law firm where you work. You've done an amazing job, and feel you have a chance this time.

The Pain of Regret is lasting. It will shape your attitude and belief in yourself, it can even reverse the course of your life. Regret is a very dangerous emotion.

It's between you and one other lawyer with a Harvard Law degree. You know how you will feel if you get passed up this time. "That one night out is going to haunt me forever!"

This story demonstrates the second kind of pain: **The Pain of Regret. It is the ugly mental anguish that we all have experienced because we didn't choose to be disciplined.** This is what I mean; you can either choose to be disciplined or choose the Pain of Regret later. As you can tell, and certainly have experienced, The Pain of Regret is lasting. It will shape your attitude and belief in yourself. It can even reverse the course of your life. Regret is a very dangerous emotion.

Discipline, by contrast, is only painful when it is happening. You get to the other side of discipline, and you feel a great sense of accomplishment. Let's say you skipped the sports bar football bash, got to bed early, woke up ready, and were on your game from the first LSAT question to the last. As you left the room, you knew you had aced that test! It would be a pretty Fantastic feeling, right? The exact opposite of regret.

You can see that in every moment of your life, you have the opportunity to choose your kind of pain. There will always be some, so which will it be? For me, I'm not perfect. I have the Pain of Regret, usually around food. My weakness is passing up plates of chocolate chip cookies and sweets, or even being disciplined enough to have just one cookie. It seems odd since, overwhelmingly, in other aspects of my life, I have trained myself to choose The Pain of Discipline nearly every time. I continue to work on my weakness and am confident I will crack the code because

I truly believe a life without regret, a life setting goals and working to achieve those goals, is exceptionally rewarding and Fantastic.

The Moment of Choice

The LSAT story is a clear-cut example of the two kinds of pain and how your choices in the moment can set you up for either a sense of accomplishment or a lot of regret later. Study, don't study. Go to the party, don't go to the party. In my case, eat four cookies, don't eat four cookies. The disciplined choices are obvious.

A lot of the time, however, the choices are not that tidy. What if you have four kids with conflicting activities? Whose baseball or softball game do you go to, and whose do you miss if they land on the same day? Which kid's team do you coach? How do you spend enough time with your partner or spouse and still spend enough time building your highly demanding career?

Everyone looks back on their lives; some may regret spending so much time at the office or missing their kid's games. Me, I spent sixty to seventy hours a week at the office for twenty-five years. I coached my kids' teams, attended their games, and spent time with my wife, Tracy. Could I have done more? Done less? Yes. But in every case, I evaluated

> ...a life setting goals and working to achieve those goals is exceptionally rewarding, and Fantastic.

what I was doing in the moment and chose my pain. I simply chose discipline and encourage you to do the same. Even when I decided to sleep in on a Saturday, it was my decision, and therefore I didn't regret that choice.

The point is that when you make a conscious choice, the likelihood of regretting that choice is virtually zero. While battling cancer several years back, friends asked me if I regretted working so many hours. It was a natural question. My answer was no, I don't regret any of that time because in the moment, I knew I was choosing discipline over regret. It was a free choice that I made. How can I be regretful of that? I can't be, and neither will you when you choose discipline over regret.

I love this quote by Brian Kight, the founder of DailyDiscipline.com. He says, "Discipline is not a possession. Discipline is a decision and an action. Discipline is not something you have; it's something you do. It's your choice." He's right. **Discipline is not something that you have. It is the way you behave, the way you live.**

Beating the Push and Pull

Have you ever met someone who decides to do one thing, does it, and then regrets not doing the other? You know, the dad who chooses to go to his son's baseball game and then finds out his daughter hit a home run with the bases loaded at her softball game the same day. He goes home, regretting that he missed his daughter's biggest game. This is The Pain of Discipline and The Pain of Regret happening together. What do you do if you find yourself in this circle of hell?

Having been in that situation many times, I've had plenty of chances to discover what works and what doesn't work. First of all, **once you make a conscious decision, you have to let it go.** "I made this decision, and I'm going to play it out." Any wavering is a recipe for a horrible life, not a Fantastic one. Second, living life looking in the rear-view mirror is a recipe for disaster. *What if I... I should have... If only I... I wish I would have...* Any sentences that start like these are dangerous to you and those around you. It's living in The Gap because you are comparing your current state to some seemingly ideal state that you missed. Yes, the Gap can happen by comparing your present to the "ideal" past that you missed, just as it can happen by comparing your present to your ideal future and how far apart they are.

Instead of setting yourself up for regret, imagine if you chose discipline. And as part of that choice, you went to the store and bought a mini tripod. You had your partner or spouse, who would be attending your daughter's game, video the whole thing on a mobile phone. Instead of regretting your choice, you could instead be reliving the grand slam over and over on video that evening. You beat the push and pull by making

The point is, when you make a conscious choice the likelihood of regretting that choice is virtually zero.

a conscious choice, doing the GRAVEL work to devise a solution, then acting on that choice with discipline. There are always solutions and alternatives, but they are hard to see when you're in a state of push-pull.

Disciplining Yourself

Earlier in my life and still today, I ask myself where in my life can I be exercising more discipline so I don't have regret later? Ask yourself that question. I constantly think about my life in terms of my true Fantastic Life and then strive towards that in a disciplined way. That means I'm naturally going to have some events I regret going to and some that I regret not going to. Just because I've chosen a different path to my Fantastic Life doesn't mean everything is hunky dory. It means that my most important things get the most time and the most action. I promise you, you will never regret focusing on your highest priority tasks.

As you begin disciplining your thoughts to choose The Pain of Discipline over The Pain of Regret, you'll find you regret less and less. Regret may not completely go away, but you'll certainly know and can choose what is important to you most of the time.

One of my business colleagues and friends is Steve Johnston. Aside from overcoming countless obstacles and building a successful software business, Platform Technology Group, in the highly challenging aviation industry, Steve underwent a physical transformation losing over fifty-five pounds in 110 days while still growing his business and tending to a very busy household with three kids under ten.

"I guess I've been living Rule #9 without even realizing it. David Goggins, who wrote the book Can't Hurt Me, is my hero. Here's a guy, a Navy Seal, who didn't buckle under Seal training 'Hell Week', which is known to be the most intense physical and mental test in the entire military. Few make it through the whole week of tests that involve, well… read the book. Even more, Goggins went on to seek out additional physical challenges that tested his own human endurance. He trained himself to seek out pain as a means of growth. While I may not seek out pain as he does, I do know that **I'm going to experience pain one way or another, so I might as well focus and get the job done, whatever that job might be. That's The Pain of Discipline, and it helped me lose fifty-five pounds and build a lot of muscle at the same time. I'm a fifty-plus-year-old guy, and I'm in the best shape of my life."**

Steve makes a good point. Pain is inevitable, so why not choose The Pain of Discipline? "That kind of pain is very short-lived," Steve says from experience. "Unlike The Pain of Regret, which you may feel for days, weeks, months, years… even forever." Steve has tracked his weight and body fat since 2006 and has lost more than twenty-five pounds seven times. His success has not been a

I promise you, you will never regret focusing on your highest priority tasks.

one-and-done story. He's battled the Pain of Discipline and the Pain of Regret over and over. "I make no excuses, but being in aviation, my travel schedule, business, and client entertaining got in the way. But I wasn't disciplined either, so as a result, I lived every day with The Pain of Regret as I watched myself pile on the weight and inch up in size."

For Steve, the only time he can work out is in the morning. "After that, I have my business so my focus has to be there. When I come home, I have family commitments. Forget it. It's exercise in the morning or not at all. Now, to me it's a priority, so I don't hit the snooze button. I mean, you keep hitting the snooze button and eventually there comes a moment when you just start to feel guilty. The Pain of Regret kicks in which is a thousand times worse than just getting up and going—The Pain of Discipline. Feeling regretful before you even get out of bed is an awful way to start the day. Anytime I've ever done that, it just makes me feel like the worst human being possible. The irony of the whole thing is that once I'm in the gym and in the groove, it feels great. That Pain of Discipline lasts just a few minutes. The Pain of Regret with the snooze button eats you up from the inside and can ruin your whole day."

He says it took the COVID-19 pandemic to create the conditions that he could actually lose the weight and keep it off. "I'm a person of extremes, and **the way I've managed The Pain of Discipline is to look past that moment of pain and know that in a few minutes, I'm going to feel great.** I actually don't like getting up in the morning, but I look past that to my pre-workout shake. Then after my workout, I'll blend up berries, fruit, almond butter, and a few other powders, and it's a great morning. No regrets to start my day."

Not a single thing in this chapter is a difficult skill. What is difficult is the discipline to take action over time. It's not hard to lift a weight over your head or jog or eat less junk food. Those are easy things to do. But like Brian Kight says, "Simple skills executed with great discipline produce powerful results." Discipline makes all the difference because discipline is the precursor to consistency, and consistency is what drives change.

Be Ready for Naysayers

Be ready for people around you to assume that just because you make a disciplined choice to do one thing, that you are falling short on something else. I've personally had people assume that because I spent so much time working, that I must have been a terrible dad. I may have worked a lot of hours, but I had and continue to have Fantastic Life goals centered on my relationships with my kids. Even when I'm tired and would rather just relax, if it's my night to call my daughter, I call her. The Pain of Discipline lasts just until I hear her voice. Then there's no pain at all; in fact, there's nothing I'd rather be doing.

> Discipline makes all the difference because discipline is the precursor to consistency and consistency is what drives change.

I share this because naysayers will use all kinds of diminishing assumptions about you as excuses for not achieving their own goals. Don't buy into it. How am I able to work so much and spend so much time with my kids? Easy. First of all, I have clarity about what's important and the life I want. That includes career, family, kids, fitness, health, and spirituality. See Rule #3 Build Your Resumes Every Year. If those naysayers had clarity in their lives, they'd instead say something like, "I think what you are choosing to do is great! I choose to do this or that." This or that may be watching 100 pro football games every season. That's great! That clarity! When you have clarity, you find you have time to do what's important.

Naysayers might also get a little passive-aggressive on you. I have encountered comments like, "Well, Craig, actually, I decided I don't want a challenging career. I just want to go to work and come home eight hours later with no worries. So I can be there for my kids," implying that I worked a grueling career, came home with worrying distractions and wasn't there for my kids. Comparing yourself or having others compare themselves to you and owning that comparison is living in The Gap. Give that up. Remember, this is your own game. And that is their own game. Set the rules of your game so you can win. If only this person would have said, "Life is good. I work eight hours and still have time to hang out with my kids, which is important to me." That's clarity, that's choice, and that's great! This guy was only trying to justify living a meager life by making me the bad guy. What is he setting himself up for? Regret. You better believe it.

And then there will be people who ask you repeatedly how you accomplished your goals. In Steve's case, his body transformation. Steve said, "I'll tell them exactly how I started and how I progressed, and it's like they don't even hear my words. They have programmed themselves to believe The Pain of Discipline is too hard. But really, to me, it's The Pain of Regret that I avoid at all costs. People get into a downward spiral because they avoid The Pain of Discipline over and over, and it plays on their psyche, feelings of self-worth, and eventually shame. It's a real trap."

The last thing I want for you is to be that person who, years down the line, says they gave up their career, or sacrificed their health, or traded in their freedom for their kids or their family or their dream. You hear it every day, and it really is sad. It's The Pain of Regret. No! **Make disciplined choices moment by moment. Identify what is important to you and what will take you further to your goals. When you discipline yourself to do this, you'll avoid this kind of pain decades later. The Fantastic Life is a disciplined life, and within that is the freedom and the means to do and be anything you want.**

The bottom line?
Choose discipline.

...naysayers will use all kinds of diminishing assumptions about you as excuses for not achieving their own goals. Don't buy into it.

Steps You Can Take

Explore your past pain Take a little time to think back to when you experienced the Pain of Discipline and the Pain of Regret. Write down how you felt in those instances. What did you give up? How long did the pain last? What did it feel like? Do your answers tell you which kind of pain is more painful?

Identify and recognize potential sacrifices Every goal that you have is going to require some sacrifice. Remember, you can do and be *anything* you want; you just can't go and be *everything* you want. So what will you have to give up to achieve your goals? Write those things down and come to terms with them. If you aren't willing to do that—like I wasn't willing with the goal of hiking from Mexico to Canada—cross out the goal. Maybe revisit it another time.

Look ahead and choose Take a look at your day, today or tomorrow, and see what's on the horizon. Where in your day will you face the two kinds of pain? Is it right when you wake up and choose to get out of bed and get some exercise? Will it be at that breakfast meeting and what you decide to eat? Or how about in the midst of your day when you have to face a difficult conversation? Make the decision now to choose the Pain of Discipline in each case and see how it feels.

9. Recognize There are Two Kinds of Pain

Thoughts

- What do you really want to accomplish in life? Now that you know some pain will be involved, does that change your goals?

- Will the sacrifices you have to make be worth it? Who will they impact, and how will you manage those relationships?

- When in the last week or two have you chosen the Pain of Discipline? How about the Pain of Regret? Are you still living with the high or the low?

- What can you do to be better at choosing the Pain of Discipline?

- Who can you enlist to help?

9. Recognize There are Two Kinds of Pain

193

the FANTASTIC LIFE revisited

The point of Rule #10,
is to help you make
better choices that become
so reflexive they aren't
choices at all.

Fantastic Life Rule
Take the Decision Out of the Moment

Eating healthy is part of my Fantastic Life, so I never look at a menu when I go to a restaurant, and not because I always order or eat the same foods. Instead, **I always look at the menu online in advance and know precisely what I'm going to order long before I sit down. I take the decision out of the moment—along with the temptation to choose something I'm going to regret eating.**

Food is my weak spot; we talked earlier about the cookies. I am so disciplined when it comes to training for my 100-mile off-trail hikes, choosing The Pain of Discipline every time. When it comes to food, I can be disciplined much of the time, but often I'm not. So, I've set up a system for business lunches, where even just one bacon-cheeseburger with fries can undermine a week's worth of healthy choices. It's a system that ensures I never walk away regretting what I ate.

I know me. And if I leave my restaurant menu decision to the moment I sit down at the table, and am starving, with all the aromas and overflowing plates passing by me, I'm likely to make a choice I will regret. By taking the decision out of the moment, I continue to work toward my fitness and wellness goals, have a satisfying lunch, and not overindulge. The point of Rule #10, Take the Decision out of the Moment, is to help you make better choices that become so reflexive that they aren't choices at all.

Here's a work-related example of taking the decision out of the moment. In commercial real estate, the best brokerage teams do what just about every brokerage team hates to do, and that is to make cold calls. Ask a hundred people in sales, and one, maybe two, might say they enjoy calling people they don't know, who aren't expecting their calls, and striking up a conversation. Furthermore, if you're a busy sales team that spends most of its time moving deals toward closing, cold calling often gets put off until tomorrow. Of course, tomorrow never comes; cold calling gets back-burnered indefinitely, and eventually, your team has a no deal pipeline.

The problem is that the decision to cold call or not to cold call is often made in the moment. "Should I take an hour and review this letter of intent (LOI) one more time and get it out the door? That's really important. Or… should I set it aside for just an hour and make twenty cold calls? Hmmm… I really want to get this LOI out. I'll just do that first, and then I'll do the cold calls." This mental dialog should sound familiar. In your world, you likely have your own version of it. And you know what happens next: The LOI review comes first and it doesn't take an hour. Issues arise that take more time. Then a call comes in that you absolutely have to take; there's an office birthday celebration at 2:00, the revised LOI final-final review.... and guess what? Your prospects are now home having dinner—no cold calling.

Getting Creative Pays Off

So what did I do for my brokerage team to move our pipeline-building cold calling to the front burner, consistently taking the decision out of the moment? First, I created a "Get Two" system where every morning first thing, everyone, including me, has to make two cold calls. That's it. Get just two calls done. It's easy, and it takes very little time. But wow, does it produce results. That's ten cold calls per person per week, and in a team of five, that totals fifty cold calls every week! Most teams don't do that in a year. This one habit removes all the call reluctance salespeople often face out of each and every day.

Once we got really proficient at our Get Two habit, I asked myself, "How can we do better than fifty cold calls a week? If that habit consistently generates business, what would happen if we did a little more?" So, I applied the 2% Rule and created our Cold Calling Contests. Once a month, we all get on a Zoom conference call and mute our audio. There we are, five of us in our little Zoom boxes, dialing away. We make our calls—as many as possible—within the one-hour time limit. We

CEDRIC CHINN SAYS: "How quickly you act after coming to a decision is just as important as how you come to said decision."

use chat to comment, poke a little fun at ourselves, laugh at some of the comments and turn what used to be the solitary business of cold calling into an entertaining group activity. At the end of an hour, the timer buzzes, and we go over our results. Who made the most dials, and who had the most meaningful calls? Who got a new business meeting? What was the funniest comment?

And we give away prizes. Who doesn't like prizes? You get the toilet trophy if you made the fewest calls, and that makes everyone laugh—the toilet gets passed around for sure. We all suck sometimes! You get a shark trophy if you make the most calls, and you get a champ trophy if you have the most meaningful call. Then there is the money incentive. I'll throw in $100 for achievements like getting the meeting, etc. We just mess around with it and keep it fun. Five of us make about twenty-five calls on average within the hour. That's an extra 125 cold calls per month. I don't need to tell you that this has made a big impact on our new business pipeline as well as our team morale. It's helpful to do this type of hard work together.

Creating Systems Helps Too

In both these work examples, **I took the decision out of the moment by creating a system with a specific activity, specific times, and specific rules that now happen automatically.** It's now just part of our workday, part of our month. It's what we do, and we never again have to think about "should I or shouldn't I" cold call. We never miss a week or a month. Our team no longer dreads cold calling, and they no longer leave for the day with the regret that they didn't choose the Pain of Discipline and just make the calls. You see how all these Rules for a Fantastic Life work together?

Have you ever heard of the term "sinking fund," and do you know what it means? One of the things I teach my kids is always to have a sinking fund—a bank account where you put aside money— for things like cars, house down payments, Christmas gifts, travel, vacations, etc. And you don't buy those things until you have the money in the sinking fund to do it. This kind of system takes the decision out of the moment and keeps you out of debt. Debt is good if it makes you money and bad if it costs you money. Credit card debt is bad debt and not at all part of a Fantastic Life.

Once you have a sinking fund mindset, the question of, "Even though we don't have the money, should we take that trip to Hawaii?" completely goes away. Too many people face this crossroads when they see that shiny object and buy it on credit because they don't have the money to pay for it. Then they're paying off that car or vacation or furniture for years; that's how they get into financial trouble. Isn't it more Fantastic and freeing to know your new convertible, that ski trip, or that chair you're sitting in is paid-in-full and truly yours?

Wake up and get going. A Fantastic Life is to be lived, not snoozed.

Accountability Partners Hold the Power

Workout buddies are another way to take the decision out of the moment. When you know you have to meet your workout partner at the gym, it's a lot harder to decide to skip a day. You go because someone is waiting for you and counting on you. Workout buddies can be two-legged, like a good friend, or four-legged, like your dog who is sitting by the door looking at you with eyes that say, "Let's go." The persistent whimper or whine is also effective. Your dog gives you no choice. It's time for a walk.

My hiking buddy and accountability partner, Brad, has taken the decision out of the moment for me many times. One of the motivators for staying dedicated to my endurance training is that on our hikes, lagging behind isn't an option. And I know I play the same role for Brad. We keep each other in check with workouts, food intake, hydration, sleep, and all the things it takes to perform at an extreme level.

A friend of mine told me she was going to do a thirty-mile Peloton bike ride as part of her training for a sixty-mile ride in the coming months. When she mentioned offhand that tonight was the night for the thirty-mile training ride, I said, "Text me afterward and let me know how it went." She didn't think anything of it and agreed. I had my reasons.

The following day, my friend texted me, saying, "Good thing you told me to text you after I did the ride. About five miles in, I thought, 'Man, this is going to be a long haul. Do I really want to do this right now? It's late... maybe just do a shorter workout today.' The mental acrobats were in full swing. Then I thought of you, Craig, and that was it. I had to finish the ride. I wasn't going to text you and tell you I quit."

My reply was, of course, congratulations for nailing the ride and hitting the goal. But I also knew that even though my friend was physically strong enough to ride thirty miles and more, she would face mental hurdles and have to overcome them. That's a big part of endurance training. That's why I said, "Text me when you're done." I wanted to take the decision out of the moment.

Goal Clarity Plays a Role

So much of this comes down to your goals and how you prioritize your life around them. My friend isn't just going to hop on that bike one day and ride sixty miles when the most she has ever ridden is twenty. No, that sixty-mile goal requires a strategy, particularly for the mental part of the ride. Well, **a strategy gets executed far more consistently if wherever and whenever possible, you take the decision out of the moment.**

For example, I have stated and written on my goal sheets every year since I've been married and had kids that in my life, my wife and children are most important. Family comes

Discipline is important, but even more important is that you are crystal clear on your goals. Often that alone takes the decision out of the moment.

first. So with that, I made the decision a long time ago that if my wife Tracy or any of my kids call me during a meeting or while on a call, I stop what I'm doing and answer their calls. No exceptions. The decision is out of the moment because if my wife and kids are truly a top priority, then why would I let their calls go to voicemail, ever?

Discipline is important, but even more important is that you are crystal clear on your goals. Often that alone takes the decision out of the moment. That's why it's easy for me to stop whatever I'm doing when my family calls. As a result, I never stress over it or worry if I angered the person I'm with or made the right choice. There's no choice; it's just what I do. I answer their calls 100% of the time. Acting on this kind of clarity is very freeing, and it's that freedom that makes for a Fantastic Life.

Knowing Your Story Helps

My friend and former client, Fred Pakis, is one of those people who has done so much in his life that it's almost as if he has lived two lives. I think he has. In his first life, he and his business partner, Jim Armstrong, started JDA Software, one of the most successful tech companies in the retail space, and now, in his second life, he devotes his time to philanthropy. When you read Fred's story, you'll see within it the role your journey plays in taking the decision out of the moment.

We are all products of our upbringing, and Fred grew up during the 1950s and 1960s in a middle-class midwestern family and town. A gifted athlete, Fred earned several college football scholarships. "My family was a military family, my dad was a WW2 veteran and my brother was at the U.S. Military Academy at West Point. So even though I had other offers, that's where I found myself as a freshman. It was a completely alien environment—adding the discipline overlay, the military overlay to this idea of college—especially for a kid who didn't want a military career.

"By my first year, I was captain of the plebe football team, and I had settled in. That is until I suffered a career-ending football injury. At that point, without football, I asked myself, what am I doing here? And with no good answer, I transferred to Case Institute of Technology at – Case Western Reserve University, a school known for engineering, back home in Cleveland.

"I've always been a person who had a sense for massive trends that were happening beyond my tiny world. That awareness played into my career, starting with my search for a path. There I was, at Case Western, and I didn't want to be an engineer any more than I wanted to be in the Army. Within a short time, I found this little-known major called Operations Research that was part electrical engineering, part library science, and part math. It was the very beginning of what we now call information technology, automation,

"...during my upbringing and my work life, I discovered my values, and they guided my decisions—in essence taking the decision out of the moment."

and computing. Thinking this is where the world is heading and actually liking my brief encounters with computers of the day, I found my major."

From there and upon graduation, Fred found himself working in Fortune 200 companies, participating in high-level meetings because he had a tool called technology and the knowledge to help executives find answers to business problems. "I was the guy with the computer, so at just twenty-four years old, I was getting exposure to business strategy and learning communications skills within the higher levels of the corporation. My thing was my ability to bridge business and technology, and it seemed everyone needed it."

In his late twenties, Fred earned his master's degree in London and moved his new wife there to live. "The whole experience was very multi-national. There were about thirty of us, and I was one of only two Americans in the program. That helped me because by my mid-thirties, after returning to the States and working five years with a Big 4 management consulting firm I realized that starting my own business was really what I wanted to do. That's when Jim Armstrong in Calgary, Alberta (Canada) and myself in Cleveland, we created JDA Software. JDA's mission was to automate all the bits and pieces of a retailer. There were a lot of retailers, and every one of them had a lot of bits and pieces."

Within two years, Fred and Jim opened a London office, and before long, JDA, headquartered in Phoenix, had offices all over the world. Fred's awareness of trends and international experience paid off. Success in the mid-90s led the company to an IPO, and instantly this private partnership became a Wall

Street tech pioneer. **"I always saw my work as a means to an end, never the end itself. So when I realized I could exit the company financially free, I took it. I was forty-five years old."** That was the closure of Fred's first life. **"It wasn't a difficult decision—maybe no decision at all actually—because I was clear on what my end goal was.** It was as if I had made this decision a long time ago." Fred had taken the decision out of the moment years before.

Fred's second life started a few years after that when he began a charitable foundation and dedicated the second half of his career to giving back. "I always knew where I wanted to go. I was never going to be that 70-year-old guy who still leads his company. That's just not me. I wanted more freedom than that. Second, during my upbringing and my work life, I discovered my values, and they guided my decisions—in essence, taking the decision out of the moment."

Values Become Beacons

It's true what Fred is saying **when you live your life focused on your goals, both what you learn and the person you become guide your decisions. Then, when you consistently operate day-to-day based on your values, many decisions you face are really non-decisions.** So how do you discover your values and make sure they are true guides in your life? Fred has insight into that.

"I'm of the philosophy that life is hard. It's complicated and sometimes dangerous. Having an ethical framework that helps you put a box around and filter all the stuff that comes flying at you is critical. Particularly if you can trust the box, the filter, it just makes your life easier, less complicated. **Without that box or filter, you're going to go through a lot of mental and emotional gyrations, wondering what to do. And in the heat of the moment, you probably won't make the best decision. Plus, there's just not enough time in the day if you have to think through everything. You have to move faster, more reflexively."** This is Fred's way of talking about values.

"My values have always been derived from my feelings. For example, what makes me feel happy? What makes me feel proud of myself? What makes me feel satisfied? And then I examine what event made me feel that way—as opposed to what made me feel embarrassed or sad, or frustrated—and I know that's the kind of thing I want more of in my life. That awareness takes many, many decisions out of the moment. It helps me go in the direction of what's important."

For Fred, taking the decision out of the moment is, in effect, acting on those feelings that come from his values. Ever hear someone say, "You have to live your values?" Well, this is living your values. If your decisions aren't reflexive "non-decisions," your values might not really be your values. "It's not about being super rigid, however, because life circumstances change and what is important to you changes as you make your way through life. It's also not about making exceptions because, say, a lot of money is involved. I go with my values and my feelings, and I trust the outcomes. That's the box, the filter, I'm talking about. It's your ethical construct that takes the decision out of the moment."

Decision Awareness

This chapter started with examples of how you can take the decision out of the moment and achieve—versus undermine—your goals. While many of the examples seemed like "in the moment" decisions, they too often have values-based foundations. For instance, if doing what you say you're going to do is one of your values, you'll likely unconsciously follow through on promises no matter how difficult or inconvenient. Because of your values, you've taken the decision out of the moment. But if follow-through isn't necessarily a value, and you're pretty good at it but not 100%, you may find yourself needing to figure out a way to take that kind of decision out of the moment. Particularly if it is impacting your Fantastic Life goals.

When you have awareness of those areas of your life that tend to undermine progress toward your goals or cause you regret, those are the ones that you can improve by figuring out a way to take the decision out of the moment.

Why not take a look at the times when you've had to make decisions and see which ones were reflexive, based on values, and which ones you made in the moment? Having that kind of awareness is **powerful.** I know food is my weakness, so I have a system. If getting exercise is a problem, get a dog that needs a walk every day. Your dog will take the decision out of the moment. When you have an awareness of those areas of your life that tend to undermine progress toward your goals or cause you regret, those are the ones that you can improve by figuring out a way to take the decision out of the moment.

Steps You Can Take

Write down your values This isn't an easy exercise because, too often our values are what we think our values should be rather than what they are. Think about, instead, those times when you felt really good about your decision and actions. What happened just before that? What made you feel that way? Was it because you helped someone in distress? (Maybe caring about others is a value?) Was it because you scored a huge account you worked really hard to win? (Maybe hard work and perseverance are values?) You get the idea. Look deeper than words like "integrity" or "doing the right thing."

10

Take the Decision Out of the Moment

Where do you need accountability partners? Are there particular areas of your life where having someone who will hold you accountable will help you take the decision out of the moment? If so, what are those areas, and whom can you recruit to do the job? It's okay, have lots of accountability partners if you want. There is no limit to the success you can achieve.

Create some systems Just like I have a system for making smarter choices at a business lunch, where can you create some systems that will take the decision out of the moment? You can really make these fun with a bit of creativity; kind of like our cold calling games. What is your version of that in your own life? I would strongly suggest you buy and read my book rocks GRAVEL sand. There are whole chapters on building systems.

11 Take the Decision Out of the Moment

Thoughts

▎ Now that you've gotten this far in the book, have you arrived at a clearer view of who you are and what you want to be remembered for in this lifetime? Big question, but one worth thinking about to guide your decisions.

▎ Now that you are discovering your real values, how can you make them more alive in your daily activities? When you do, your decisions become reflexive non-decisions.

▎ How will this prepare you for the bigger life decisions that will inevitably come your way? What are they, and how will you respond?

//
10

Take the Decision Out of the Moment

the FANTASTIC LIFE® revisited

Carving up your 24 hours and not wasting time, first and foremost, takes clarity about what's important to you.

Fantastic Life Rule
Don't Waste Time

When I say don't waste time, I mean don't spend time doing things that aren't important to your Fantastic Life goals. Period. Implied in that directive is that you have clarity about what is important to you. Instead, spend time on those activities that get you closer to your goals. That way, no matter what you're doing during your day, you'll know it is worthwhile and not a waste of time. I created this rule to help me always focus on my Fantastic Life and my goals.

We just talked about taking the decision out of the moment in the last chapter. There are few time wasters as potent as indecision. Flip-flopping between I will or I won't, should I or shouldn't I, taking one path then backtracking the other way. A Fantastic Life has no time for that. That's why being mindful of the time you spend and how you spend it is so important. It's no fun being mired in indecision, and it's no fun spinning your wheels on pointless activities.

If you're like most people who I share this rule with, you're looking back at your typical day and thinking, "When you put it like that, I think I waste a lot of time." That's okay. This is a new concept, perhaps for you. Think of those hours you waste and will eventually put to good use, as found time, as opportunities for you to achieve your goals. You have time to reallocate! You're not tapped out! That's great news!

Let's face it, wasting time sometimes can feel pretty good in the moment. "I deserve a break. Let me just check my Instagram." Then two hours later, with the afternoon pretty much shot, you think, "Crap, I just wasted two hours. Now there's no time to exercise because I have a conference call in ten minutes, and after that, I need to pick up the kids from school." Makes you feel pretty bad, right? Even worse is spending hours a week on TikTok or binge-watching TV shows and NOT feeling bad about it. These are not part of my Fantastic Life.

Wasting time is just another area of our lives where we come face to face with the Pain of Discipline versus the Pain of Regret. And who wants regret? That's not a Fantastic Life at all. A Fantastic Life *is* knowing what you want and going after it deliberately, mindfully, and with passion throughout the day. And feeling good when you put your head on your pillow each and every night that you "got the win" and crushed your day. **When you set your life up to use time toward those things that are important to you, you'll never have to question whether or not you're wasting time. You'll know that you aren't.**

We All Have the Same 24

You and me, we both have the same 24-hour day. For me, it's all about allocating my day based on my goals—those things that are important to me. So if I say I'm going to sleep seven hours a night, which is now important to me after my bout with cancer, and I'm going to work eight to nine hours a day, that leaves me seven or eight hours a day to do those other things that I care about. Given that I'm very clear about my Fantastic Life goals, I know I'll use up at least twenty-one hours in my day. Between sleeping, working, spending time with my wife and family, exercising, and wellness, I might have an hour or two of so-called "free time." During my day, if what I'm doing advances those goals, I never question my use of time. Spending time with my family, working on my business, working out and exercising, and reading books, I've made all those decisions up front, and I know they're a good use of my time.

Carving up your 24 hours and not wasting time, first and foremost, takes clarity about what's important to you. Then **look at your 24 in terms of two chunks of time. The first chunk is the biggest, and it includes doing things that matter in your life.**

If you have clarity and welcome the Pain of Discipline, you're probably able to take the decision out of the moment, and you plow through that part of your day.

TONY ROBBINS SAYS:

"Remember, in life, we all get what we tolerate."

As I mentioned earlier, for me, that's about twenty-one hours of my day that's planned based on what's important to me. No regrets.

The second chunk is what's left. That may be more than an hour, and that's good. It gives you time to allocate toward your goals. For me, that time is for reading, relationships, organization, and preparation. That leads to two possible actions: First, **how can I be more efficient during my first chunk of time**, shaving off minutes or hours to put toward something that matters to me? And next, **how can I allocate that second chunk of time more effectively? This is how you stop wasting time.**

Plan to Get to What's Important

At this point in reading this chapter, there's no need to wait. You can take a few actions right off the bat. First, you can make sure you have clarity about your goals (more *GRAVEL* work). You can look at how you spend your 24 hours and ask yourself, how much of that time are you spending doing what's most important to you? You can look at your free time and ask, "What other better use might I have for that time?" And where can you start chiseling time off to free up even more time to do the things important to you? **When you carve up your day like this and have an awareness of how you spend your time, you'll perhaps see for**

the first time how some people seem to have more than 24 hours in their day. They don't, of course. They just don't waste the 24 they have.

I do this little efficiency exercise regularly and, over the years, have gotten many daily tasks whittled down, freeing up hours in my day. That's because I've been managing my time this way for decades. For example, when I started thinking this way, I was working too many hours and not taking enough time for other areas of my life. It wasn't at all Fantastic, and that's why something had to change. I still had the same workload and knew that to achieve my financial goals now and for the future, reducing that wasn't an option. I realized I had to get more efficient and free up time that I was wasting. And there were plenty of opportunities to do that.

You'll have plenty of opportunities, too, particularly if you haven't thought of your day in this very deliberate way. Our days are full of classic time wasters, so in the beginning, you'll be able to shave off hours of wasted time. When it comes to your free time, with clarity of your Fantastic Life goals, you'll be a wise allocator of that time and rid yourself of worthless activities.

> **Our days are full of classic time wasters and in the beginning, you'll be able to shave off hours of wasted time.**

Classic Time Wasters

Worthless activities. We all have them in our day. And worst of all, they often masquerade as necessary. **When you start to look at your day in terms of what's really important and throw out all those pre-conceived notions of "non-negotiables," you'll be shocked by how much time you can save and allocate toward achieving your Fantastic Life goals.**

Here's one big time waster you may think is completely out of your control: commuting to and from anywhere. Maybe you can move closer to the office, airport, or places you frequent. That would cut down on time. But most likely, that may be years in the future, if at all. So what do you do? You figure out ways to work toward your goals while on the road. If one of your goals is to learn a foreign language, find a podcast and practice in the car. If you want to read fifty books a year—I have a book goal—listen to audiobooks in traffic. Many people do. If you want to eat better and get healthy, use that time to learn about nutrition. The point is, your commute time doesn't have to be just sitting there listening to music or depressing news.

And if you commute by train or bus, wow! Your world of opportunities really opens up to take on what's important. Don't waste that valuable time playing video games or hanging out on social media unless they are among your Fantastic Life goals, and I hope neither are. Instead, why not write that book, knit that scarf, design your new home— whatever your goals are. If fitness is a goal, rather than drive, can you walk to work? Run? Bike? As you can see, wasting time commuting is not a given. You can do more and be more during that hour or two of your day. I think you are better than a social media addiction and have way more to offer the world and give yourself.

Here's another time waster: Getting ready in the morning. Many people spend forty-five minutes to an hour or more on their daily routine. I have one friend who became so frustrated with how long it was taking her to get out the door one morning that she counted the steps in the process. Between opening bottles, pouring out shampoo, wringing out washcloths, putting away hairbrushes... it was over 200 steps! Lots of room for carving off wasted activities, and she did, saving herself a half hour every day. That's ten hours per work week, 520 hours a year! What can you do with that kind of time? Learn a new language, get in the best shape of your life, read the classics, make ten new friends, start a business, etc.

I can get ready in fifteen minutes because I have built-in efficiencies and have taken the decision out of the moment. For example, I only have black socks. They go with everything. And I always wear a white or blue shirt and slacks. Again, no time spent deciding. Why? Because wardrobe isn't important to me. If dressing well is important to you, figure out how to make that aspect of your life more efficient. Or make other areas of your life—the ones you don't care about—more efficient, so you

Yes this is part organization, but it is also decision fatigue avoidance. Not only do these little details suck time away from your day, they suck the energy away too.

have more time to spend on clothes. The hours in your day are finite, so what is your ideal? What are your Fantastic Life trade-offs?

Steve Jobs always wore a black mock turtleneck, Simon Cowell a white tee-shirt. Their choices were for efficiency, but their consistency made those "non-decisions" part of their trademark looks. You may think this is a little over the top, but have you ever just gotten plain overwhelmed by the number of decisions you make in a day? Big and small? If so, you're not alone. It's called decision fatigue, and the byproduct of it is inefficiency and ineffectiveness, which lead to not achieving the things in life you want. Literally, too many decisions just overwhelm us, possibly to the point of us doing nothing. We completely freeze up.

Make Efficiency a Game

Getting more efficient doesn't have to be excruciating. Actually, it can be a competitive sport! My buddy and I would go hiking every morning. So that we could stay on the mountain longer, he'd let me take a shower at his house before going to work. After our hike, I'd drive to his house, and he would always go to Starbucks, one mile away, for his first cold brew. The game I'd play was, can I be showered, shaved, and out the door before he came back with his coffee? After honing my routine, about 50% of the time, I'd be showered, shaved, and locking his door before his car pulled into the driveway.

That's the kind of efficiency—and the kind of time—that you can get when you think about what's important. Think about that. I'm picking up an extra 20-30 minutes of time every morning compared to my hiking buddy. Add to that my speed getting out the door. That's five extra hours per week of productive work time. Do you think that could make a difference financially?

I won't pick on people who watch TV shows because I get it; there is a lot of excellent stuff out there. *Billions* was one of the shows I wanted to watch, but I didn't want to lose the time. So, I only watched it while I was riding the Peloton bike. That was over fifty one-hour rides. More than 40,000 calories expended. This is what I mean. Don't waste time.

If you like to compete with yourself or against the clock, this should be a natural strategy for you. And a rewarding one because taking wasted time and turning it into productive or free time is like getting a gift. A gift that pays dividends!

Wasted Time Versus Free Time

So is the goal to not waste any time, or is the goal to have some free time? There's a vast difference between wasted time and free time. And to be clear, the goal is to have no wasted time; it's not to have no free time. There is a distinction.

...have you ever just gotten plain overwhelmed by the number of decisions you make in a day? Big and small? If so, you're not alone. It's called decision fatigue and the byproduct of it is inefficiency and ineffectiveness...

Wasted time is time you spend doing things that don't matter to you and that don't advance your Fantastic Life goals. Free time is time that you can use to do what's important to you. That can be anything. And in any given week, you may use your free time to read, chill, push forward, make more business calls, take your dog to the park, visit the grandkids, chat with your sister on the phone, get extra sleep, whatever.

By eliminating wasted time, you'll find you have a lot more free time than you thought. That's good because now you can put that time to better use. The idea is to have no wasted time and all the free time you want and need based on your goals. For example, I do my push-ups every morning and in between sets is a perfect time to read a page or two of a book. I need to recover physically, and reading helps. By using my recovery time wisely, I have more free time.

A friend of mine who works out plays with her dog in between sets. That way, she gets her workout in and gives her dog some play time too. Everyone is happy. The trick is to look for compatible activities that make your life and the time you spend more efficient. When you do that, you have more free time to use as you please.

Some people can laugh at this way of organizing your 24 hours. They are also the ones who say they don't have time to work out, eat healthy foods, go on vacation, or... fill in the blank... They do have time; they just aren't using the time they have to get the stuff done that matters. And that's the root of the problem: they don't have clarity about what's important to them. They just blow in the wind. Again my 24 and your 24 and your friend's 24 are all the same. It's how we choose to use that 24 that is different.

The Little Things Matter

The best part of this rule is that the little things matter. They matter because they add up, and that math sucks time out of your day. For example, I don't waste time looking for things. I don't look for reading glasses, for paper clips, for highlighters. Yes, I am reading five books that I highlight, so I have a highlighter in every book. Reading glasses are in drawers in most rooms because that's where I use them. Another friend I know has garden clippers in the front of her house and in the back, so no matter where she is, she can just grab the clippers and trim whatever is needed. No more walking to the garage and back—wasting time.

No one I know likes spending time on mundane tasks, particularly those that can be done in a third of the time with a little forethought and organization. I asked Chelsea and Stefanie (my assistants) if they would go through all my camping gear because they love to organize. Now it's all labeled and in order. This means I can literally get ready to go backpacking for a one- or two-night trip in twenty minutes. And when I'm done, I can unpack just as quickly because everything has its place. The decision is out of the moment.

The trick is to look for compatible activities that make your life and the time you spend more efficient...

Yes, this is part organization, but it is also decision fatigue avoidance. Not only do these little details suck time away from your day, they suck the energy away too. Too much decision clutter, too much mind clutter, and you have no energy to do the things that matter to you.

The most important thing—and I know I'm really driving this point home in this chapter especially—is you want to get complete clarity on your Fantastic Life big rock goals. Only then can you look at those goals and decide what will give you a major return on investment of your time. Finally, let's have some fun and make a game out of becoming really effective in decreasing your activity time.

How About an Extra Hour?

One of the first things we do with our entry-level commercial brokerage team members, or "runners" as they are called, is teach them not to waste time. When we teach them how to get out the door in the morning efficiently, we save them, on average, at least an hour of their life every single day. Some save that just on their commute times alone. From day one, we have them track and time their commute. Over a month, they find out the best times to make the commute coming into the office and going home. We *always* save them time on this one process alone. We get others on our team in the "don't waste time" mindset, too. For people who used to spend thirty minutes at breakfast and another twenty-five minutes showering and forty minutes in traffic, we show them how to be at the office in forty-five minutes. That's just the start of their journey. From there, those who embrace this example and apply it to other areas of their lives have gone on to achieve far more than the average person. That's because they have removed time-wasting activities from their day.

I've talked about making cold calls many times in this book. When we have our cold calling contests, we don't waste time looking for names and phone numbers. We have our call sheets prepared with all the information we need. That hour is for making calls, not researching the people we want to call. That would be a waste of that hour. When the clock starts, we're ready to make calls.

Part of the secret of not wasting time is being ready. For so much of your day, you know what you're going to face, right? Why not be prepared? In advance, so that the time you spend on those tasks is minimal. There are thousands of little ways you can shave off the minutes that become hours in your day. Be committed to your goals and find those ways to free up time to attain them.

How many times have you said, "Oh, I want to take time off, but I haven't had a very productive week, so I can't go." I can tell you I don't ever want to do that. I don't ever want to be that person. The freedom to take time off is a byproduct of not wasting time. I've heard people say that procrastination means you

"Challenging yourself every day is one of the most exciting ways to live."

just haven't committed yet. Maybe there is some truth to that. But I don't want any procrastination in my life. It's a time waster.

You Won't Believe What You Can Achieve

My friend and business associate Steve McConnell is an excellent example of what we're talking about. From the time he was a kid, he knew that wasting time was, well, a waste. "I grew up with fabulous parents, in Boston. I went to Belmont Hill High School, to Harvard College, and then to Harvard Business School. I could have taken time in between, but I didn't. I knew what I wanted to do, so I wanted to get out there and do it."

Steve was a hard worker, even in his teens. "I enjoyed working, which taught me how to be efficient and productive with my time. It provided me with contacts, friends, money, and opportunities that I would never have had otherwise."

When Steve graduated, he entered into what today would be called Private Equity, and he was working to raise capital to buy businesses. "A few positions and many deals later, I decided I wanted to work for myself. So, in 1990 I took the leap. Even though I had been a part of some very big deals, I didn't have a lot of money. But with the money I had, I went out and immediately bought two businesses. They worked, so I bought a few more businesses—managing some—and over the last thirty years, I've done at least 350 different deals where I am my own private equity."

Once in charge, Steve was able to run his firm according to his own values, and one of them was never to waste time. Part of the reason was that efficiency positively impacted the success of the company, but also because Steve had other interests—demanding interests—that were a part of his daily life. "Staying healthy is a principle that is important to me. And that takes time. I was a marathon runner, and I exercised almost every single day. There is nothing more important than maintaining good health and staying sharp. Exercise does that, and because I'm smart about how I spend my day, I have time for that."

Steve gets asked all the time, "How can you hold over 50 ownership positions and still have time to exercise and stay fit?" His answer is a pure example of how he spends his time doing what's important to him. He gets rid of tasks that interfere with his health goals because he says the biggest time waster is getting sick.

"I wake up in the morning, I brush my teeth, get a little something to eat, and I go exercise. I enjoy it. Staying healthy is so critical. I mean, when you get sick, it just, totally throws you off the rails. So, it makes sense to work to stay healthy and, you know, extend the runway."

Another aspect of life important to Steve is his relationships, which, again, take time. "The Golden Rule is so important to me because why wouldn't you treat people like you want to

MICHAEL ALTSCHULER SAYS:

"The bad news is time flies. The good news is you're the pilot."

be treated? We've all been treated badly at some time in the past, and it didn't feel very great. Why should I turn around and treat someone else that way? I'm constantly in touch with a lot of people who are meaningful to me, and it's that social interaction that keeps you in the game. But again, that takes time, so I make sure I have enough. That's important to me."

You may be like Steve and have varied interests. For him, it's business, fitness, helping friends and charities, social connections, and of course, family. That's a pretty full plate. **He's figured out how to spend his time focused on those things and very little else. It truly is the secret for having what others might think is "more time in your day." But it's really not more time, it's a better use of time—spent on the things you love, and isn't that a Fantastic way to live? Isn't that a Fantastic Life?**

Steps You Can Take

Take a detailed look at your 24 and become a time sleuth What does your day look like? Map it out—how long do you sleep, how long does it take to get ready, to commute? How much do you work? What occupies your time in between? Track your time on social media, watching TV, etc. When you look at your day this way, you may be surprised at how much time you spend doing things that don't have anything to do with the life you want to live.

11

Don't Waste Time

Carve it up 🖊 Now take that same day and carve it up based on your goals. How would you allocate that time if you could shape your day? I bet it would be different. This will help you see the kind of day that is possible and what kind of day you'd prefer. Opportunities may come in giant leaps at first and then in smaller increments, but they will be visible.

Find time savings 🖊 Where can you save time in your day to reallocate to activities that matter? This is the exciting part of the whole thing because you'll discover how some people seem to have more hours in their day than everyone else. You'll become one of those people because you have discovered the secret of time and how to accomplish more in your day.

Create games 🖊 Where in your day can you make saving time a game? Watch TV shows, like I do, on the Peloton or treadmill. Read while you stretch. Call someone important while commuting. Can cleaning up the kitchen after dinner be a race against the clock? Would it make sense to monitor your daily walk, quicken the pace and shave off time so you can add a little strength training to your day? Find ways to challenge yourself and gamify time management.

11

Don't Waste Time

 Thoughts

▐ We all have classic time wasters in our lives. What are yours?

▐ Are you really clear on your goals? Is that how you want to spend your 24 hours? Goals get very real at this point.

▐ Is what you are doing important to you? Ask yourself that question regularly during the day and answer truthfully.

▐ Ask yourself often, "What is a better use of my time right now?"

11

Don't Waste Time

the FANTASTIC LIFE revisited

Rule #12 contradicts the shared wisdom of "everything in moderation." People who really win in life, meaning they attain all they set out to do, don't go for those dreams in moderation.

Fantastic Life Rule 12
Do Nothing in Moderation

I saved this rule for last. Do Nothing in Moderation only becomes relevant after you know all the other Rules.

1. You know and can reference all your stories.
2. You are crystal clear on what you want out of your Fantastic Life.
3. You know the resumes you want to build.
4. You know where you can play to win.
5. You get wins all day long.
6. You have goals written, dissected, and all spelled out with GRAVEL.
7. You know how to get out of The Gap.
8. You think about and use the 2% Rule all the time.
9. You understand The Pain of Discipline and The Pain of Regret.
10. You have taken all the decisions out of the moment.
11. And, you simply don't waste time.

Now you are ready for my last rule:

12. Do Nothing in Moderation.

You may have heard the saying that the best time to plant a tree was twenty years ago. The second-best time is today. **If you want something in life, go for it today with energy. You don't need to take two years to accomplish what you can do in six months if you just put in the effort and the time.** It's really hard to get Fantastic results from a quarter effort. Or no effort.

Despite how the optics appear in the news and blogs about Hollywood celebrities, YouTubers, rappers, and sports figures, they work their asses off. It might look like their life is one big party and one big photo opp, but that is not the case. They never rest. If they're not performing, they're thinking about performing, learning how to get better, finding new partnerships and mentors, writing, rehearsing, negotiating deals, fending off lawsuits, riding on a bus from one town to the next, showing up at star-studded events... Yes, that's work too, and it never ends.

Rule #12 contradicts the shared wisdom of everything in moderation. People who really win in life, meaning they attain all they set out to do, don't go for those dreams in moderation. That's almost laughable when you think about it. Don't believe me? These quotes show that Rule #12 is alive in the best of the best, alive in the people who achieve absolute greatness.

Eliud Kipchoge, the only human to finish a marathon in under two hours, says, "The celebration stops at the finish line." He says it because he is so focused, he doesn't celebrate in the traditional sense. His life, and the doing is the celebration.

After he wins, he's on to training for the next race. Kobe Bryant said, "We are obsessive when you care about something 24 hours a day." Steve Jobs said, "I'm convinced that about half of what separates the successful entrepreneurs from the non-successful ones is pure perseverance." "Unmitigated daily discipline in all things." That line comes from Jocko Willink. David Goggins makes the point by saying, "Choose to be uncommon amongst uncommon people." And lastly, "Anything in life worth doing is worth outdoing. Moderation is for cowards." This is from an unknown but wise source.

Anyone successful in life is making things happen just about 24/7 because that's what it takes. They do nothing in moderation. Have you ever seen an Olympic athlete, a Superbowl quarterback, not give their all? If you have, the likelihood is that they did not come out on top.

I'm not picking on people new to business, but I have a very long list of people who said they wanted to be part of our brokerage team and couldn't cut it. Not because they weren't smart. They were super smart and full of potential. The trouble was they lived and worked—especially worked—in moderation, which doesn't fit with our team or me. Somehow they were under the impression that a half effort in the Superbowl of life gets you the championship ring. It doesn't. And for every person who believes that

The sooner you learn to do nothing in moderation, the better off you'll be because you'll quickly leapfrog your peers, particularly if you're just starting in your career.

lie, there are others who are dying for a chance to enter the championship. Competition in life is pretty steep, particularly as you grow in your career. The stakes only get higher.

The sooner you learn to do nothing in moderation, the better off you'll be because you'll quickly leapfrog your peers, especially if you're just starting your career. **I love the saying that success is where opportunity and preparedness collide. Well, being prepared to me is doing everything you can to be in the best possible position when opportunity presents itself.** You have to show up all the time *and* give your all, plus 2%. Remember the 2% Rule? That's a very big part of doing nothing in moderation.

The Reputation You Earn

When you go for it in life, developing a reputation for being a stand out doesn't take long. That's because so many people just muddle through. They may show up, but they just don't realize that's not enough. **The adage that showing up is 80% of success might be true for those who habitually don't show up, but for those of us who do and who want to live life in the top 1% of achievers, showing up isn't enough.**

My reputation is that I am an endurance athlete in life. Whether I'm striving to achieve work goals or wellness goals or family goals, whatever, I am going to give it my all plus 2%. My son, who has started running ultra-marathons, is beginning to understand the commitment it takes to do that well, and he is excelling. I'm really proud of him. It takes a lot of dedication and certainly a commitment to banish moderation from the equation. When I was running marathons and ultra-marathons, there was a span of about fifteen years where if someone said, "Let's run a marathon today," I could have done it, no problem. Today, it's backpacking. I am prepared and able to do a ten-hour hike with a pack on any given day. You can get to that place in life for whatever activity matters to you when you do nothing in moderation as you attack your goals.

It comes back to the limits we place on ourselves and the Pain of Discipline. Doing nothing in moderation means breaking through your barriers. And once you do, you'll gain a reputation for being strong, tough, and disciplined because it will show in your work, your behavior, and in your body make-up, including your demeanor. People will wonder how you do the hard things you do. You can answer simply, "Because I do nothing in moderation."

What About Everything in Moderation?

It's popular to believe that everything in moderation is the way to go. I don't think this is true at all. **Moderation gets you nowhere. And it can be dangerous.** First, anything that is bad for your health done in moderation is still

> Doing nothing in moderation means breaking through your barriers.

bad for your health. You don't want to smoke in moderation or do drugs in moderation or drive recklessly in moderation. No, you want to avoid those things and many others that are harmful to you without moderation—meaning you want to avoid them entirely.

Moderation is a myth. If you eat ice cream in moderation, and jelly donuts in moderation, and corn dogs in moderation and expect to lose weight, avoid diabetes and prevent a future heart attack, you're going to be disappointed. If you want to avoid a lifetime of chronic illness, you must do nothing in moderation. In this case, you must be a zealot at banishing those and other unhealthy foods from your daily menu, even if you were only eating them "in moderation." Trust me on this one. I speak as someone who is still working on it.

A friend of mine learned to ski when she was 57, an age when many people decide to *quit* skiing. Did she commit to ski and then approach it in moderation? Hell, no. Moderation while learning to ski means injury. Instead, she approached it like a mission. She took lessons from the best—her instructor's son is on the U.S. Ski Team—followed the instruction to the letter then committed the time to practice what she learned until muscle memory made skiing as comfortable as walking.

After that, she took more lessons and skied more days with experienced skiers who both challenged and guided her, eventually skiing nearly thirty days a season just so that she could become confident, controlled, and highly skilled. Did she do it because she was training for the next downhill competition or because she wanted to ski double blacks? No, she did it because she wanted to truly and thoroughly enjoy her time on the slopes and skiing with others. That meant being skilled, strong, and confident. *And* she kept up her regular strength workouts even on ski days. No moderation. Yes, she has a reputation as a badass! Well-earned and cherished.

Choose Your Excess

If you do nothing in moderation when it comes to the things that matter, you'll have to say, "No," to the things that don't. Remember, you can do anything; you just can't do everything. That's why this rule is last. You must have complete clarity of your goals, resumes, and what's most important to you.

For example, I no longer scuba dive. I will not be the guy who goes on vacation and does a "scuba day." If I'm going to scuba dive, I will go for it like my friend did with skiing. I deliberately choose those things I do in excess, just as I deliberately choose those things I don't do at all—the things that don't interest me or are unimportant. Scuba diving is one of them. So on a beach vacation, you'll find me hiking in the mountains, not diving off the back of a boat. My friend who skis won't spend even a minute on the back of a Harley-Davidson on a weekend ride. Not a chance. Why risk an injury that would keep her from skiing, which she loves?

GEORGE PATTON SAYS:

"A good plan, violently executed now, is better than a perfect plan next week."

I'm also no longer the guy who will stay up late and watch the football or basketball game. I follow University of Arizona basketball. At this writing, they're ranked number 3 in the nation, and the other night, they were playing fifth-ranked UCLA. Game time started in Arizona at 9:00 pm. Did I watch one minute of the game? No. Why? Because I wanted to get up at 4:00 am to ride the Peloton bike and do the rest of my morning training. That day, I rode the bike for an hour, did my strength training, washed my car, and was at my desk before 7:30. All because I didn't watch the U of A game. Sure, I missed some stuff. I missed the game. Big deal. I can watch the highlights. I could have recorded the whole thing and watched it on my Peloton ride if it mattered—I don't waste time.

This is the perfect place to point out that **your personal "nothing in moderation" is your own choice.** A client of mine is also a big U of A fan, and there is no moderation in his fandom! That's Fantastic because U of A basketball is important in his life. He stayed up really late to watch the conclusion of that game. I'm not here to judge what your choices are. I'm here to say, have clarity, make your choice and go for it. This is *your* Fantastic Life.

Except when it comes to spending time staring at your phone on social media. Unless that is how you earn your living, I will make the judgment that there are better ways to spend your time. The statistics show that the average American now spends seven hours a day staring at a screen of some sort: their computer, mobile phone, iPad, or TV, with the vast majority of that on social media. I challenge that excess. To me, it is like an opioid. Life is happening; decide to be a part of it rather than a viewer of it. Choose something and go for it.

One last interesting fact. **Did you know that when there's a storm, cows will run away from it? But buffalos will run into it. The idea is that the buffalos get to blue skies faster. They take the storm by the horns, so to speak.** No moderation in sight, and as a result, the challenge of the storm lasts half as long as it does for the cows, which take a more moderate approach. How often do you run into the storm to get through it faster?

Moderation Trade-offs

In the last chapter, we talked about the importance of not wasting time. You learned that most of my 24 hours are allocated to doing the things that are important to me. Figuring out how to fit everything in will be tricky. And priorities change. That is why I wrote *rocks GRAVEL sand*. Because it covers what I call life's "messy middle," which is the work between your big rock goals and the sand, which are your daily tasks. Doing that GRAVEL work makes the tasks meaningful enough to cut moderation out of the equation.

If you do nothing in moderation when it comes to the things that matter, you're going to have to say, "No," to the things that don't.

I mentioned change, and a big one for me was when I decided that getting enough sleep every night is a priority. For decades I trained myself to sleep just three or four hours a night. Then I got cancer, and after my bout with it, I decided that sleeping seven hours every night was one of my goals. Now I no longer sleep in moderation—I get a full seven to seven-plus hours every night. But, wow, by committing to that goal, I lost between three and four hours I used to spend on other things that mattered. Instead of dialing back all my other goals to a place of more moderation so I could get more sleep, I asked myself, "What do I have to do to make up those hours?" The answer came back: I had to eliminate the "cushion" I used to have. Cushion, for example, might be staying up late and watching that U of A game. It used to work because sleep wasn't important to me. I didn't care how much I slept. Now I do.

The answer is all about the math. I still don't do the things that matter in moderation; I just cut out all the BS that doesn't matter. When I did that, I got much of those three hours back. Once again, I now practice no moderation in anything that matters.

You also have to do the math to make sure that the goals you have in all the areas of your life are getting your attention. Remember, the Fantastic Life isn't a life with one primary focus and then everything else gets neglected and falls apart. It's the opposite. The Fantastic Life is about achieving all the things in life that are important to you. Doing nothing in moderation is part of your arsenal to accomplish that.

I understand the need to focus on urgent goals and priorities. Getting to the pinnacle of anything in life requires a huge commitment. That is the story of my commercial real estate career. My 25 years of working 70 hours a week is doing nothing in moderation. But it didn't happen at the expense of everything else. During that time, I stayed married (in a happy marriage), raised four kids (all successful and launched), and still had time to hit all my athletic achievement goals. It's not because I'm superhuman; it's because I knew what I wanted and did nothing in moderation to get it. It has been done and can be done again. This time, by you. Follow the blueprint in this book. Make it your blueprint and execute.

Fitting the Profile

Putting all these pieces together and then executing them without moderation is powerful. One of my favorite people living the no-moderation life is Mike Lipsey, and he's been a trainer, consultant, and successful commercial real estate professional for more than forty years. He's literally been at the heart of the growth of our modern-day America. Mike's trained and coached the best in the business at all the major commercial real estate firms, Cushman Wakefield, Colliers, Coldwell Banker, and my firm, Lee & Associates, as well as others since 1981. He did not go into his business

The Fantastic Life is about achieving all the things in life that are important to you. Doing nothing in moderation is part of your arsenal to accomplish that.

in moderation. Mike went into it believing that his firm, The Lipsey Company, would own their aspect of commercial real estate. And they do.

"I think people who work out really heavily or work really hard, and do things with little moderation, it's because they have something competitive going on inside," Mike speculated about others and about himself. "I love it when my clients call me on Saturdays because they say, 'Mike, I can't believe you answered the phone.' And I tell them, I'm nine-one-one. Our office is open more than the emergency room at a level one trauma hospital. We are always open. I'm that way about my business because I believe when a client or prospect needs us, we need to be available."

Mike made it perfectly clear, "You want to work for The Lipsey Company? Well, I'm here from 7 to 7. And I'll be surprised if you're not here from 7 to 7 every day. I also like to work a half day on Saturday. I'm telling you this so before you take this job, you know what's expected. To this day, when past employees who have moved on to great success call me, they say, 'Hey, 7-to-7, how's it going?' and we laugh. But they also tell me that the work ethic they learned as college grads at The Lipsey Company was foundational to their career success. I'm glad to have played that role."

Mike has trained and coached so many people that he knows the kind of person with the best shot at success, at least in a commercial real estate commission sales position. **"I can tell you that college athletes who excelled in their sport and had to balance school work, practices, maybe even a job and get decent enough grades** to play, those are the people who do well. It's because they had to focus and really go for it. That's balance plus discipline. People who don't do well are the ones who want balance and lack discipline. They roll in at 8:45, leave at 4:00, and waste time during the day. They go hungry in our world."

You Can't Train Discipline

Lead a Fantastic Life, and you often live a life that leaves an indelible mark on others. In other words, you change people's lives. And Mike has done that with tens of thousands of people he has managed, coached, and trained. Mike, however, believes that while you can teach skills and best practices, you can't train discipline.

He's right, and that's why we have the 12 Rules that give you your action list and next steps. What will come out of incorporating and practicing these Rules are outcomes that will keep you going. Even when life hits you hard, these Rules are what will drive your inner discipline. We are not teaching discipline in the Fantastic Life. It is a byproduct of practicing the Rules and winning. Who doesn't want to keep winning?

Follow the blueprint in this book. Make it your blueprint and execute.

Even today, in a society that speaks of moderation, the fact is that achievement doesn't come from that. People say they want a balanced life. I fully believe living a Fantastic Life is all about balance. Here is balance in a Fantastic Life: Live the Rules! Get clarity, set goals, find things that are important to you and then go for them without moderation. That *is* a balanced life. Too many people think a balanced life is working some and then doing whatever they want to do, whenever. That's called a lack of discipline, not balance. That may make you feel "happy" in the moment, but will that strategy set you up for the life you want to live? In the long run, no, it won't. In the long run, will you regret those wasted years?

Mike recognizes today the importance of having more than one focus and admits he has been mostly business-minded throughout his life. He doesn't regret it, though, because he chose that life and has gotten great satisfaction knowing he was helping so many people in the commercial real estate profession be successful. And he still loves doing it.

When we talked, Mike closed with a powerful story about a trainer he met at a conference decades ago while in his twenties. That trainer said, "Mike, the thing you need to appreciate in life is that you're going to pay the price one way or the other. One way is you're going to come home at a reasonable time. You're going to open up a beer and sit in your Lazy Boy chair and watch television. Now, you won't be able to provide everything that you would like to for your family, but at least you'll be home early, and that's your price. Or, you will find a career, and you'll work at it harder than anyone else. You won't be home, you won't be getting in the Lazy Boy, and you won't be opening up the beer. However, you will be financially successful, and you will be able to provide the best for your family. You will be able to get them to the best schools, and you'll be able to give them a head start. Which means that maybe they'll achieve more than they would have, had you been the dad that came home at four o'clock. You're paying the price one way or the other."

"To this day, I can remember hearing his story sitting at this little cocktail table. That lesson stuck with me and shaped my life."

So it's true. **You may not be able to teach discipline, but you can inspire it, and you can provide the system to bring it to life and practice it.** That's *The Fantastic Life Rules*, and now you have all 12. What are you going to do with all that? The choice is yours.

Lead a Fantastic Life and you often live a life that leaves an indelible mark on others. In other words, you change people's lives.

Steps You Can Take

Get very specific Now, with all the information you have, it's time to specifically determine those things you will do with no moderation. With all 12 Rules under your belt, you know it means choosing the Pain of Discipline, not wasting time, doing 2% more, going for wins, etc. What aspects of your life are you willing to take on without moderation? What does *your* Fantastic Life look like?

Assemble your tracking system You have your goals, you have your dedication, you know what your time commitments look like, and you might even have an idea of how you will optimize your day. It's time to set up how you will hold yourself accountable.

Seize your Fantastic Life day by day Today is the first day to begin your Fantastic Life. No point wasting time; seize the moment and put the Rules into action.

12 Do Nothing in Moderation

FANTASTIC Thoughts

the FANTASTIC LIFE® revisited

■ Think about where you are and where you will be in a year. Instead of worrying about the destination, revel in the progress and the wins you achieve every day. Live the Fantastic Life. It's the journey called living, not the end.

Oscar Wilde says:

"Moderation is a fatal thing. Nothing succeeds like excess."

12 Do Nothing in Moderation

the FANTASTIC LIFE® revisited

Consistency is the magic bullet that everyone looks for but few want to admit is absolutely critical to any kind of success.

Chapter 13
Consistency

Now you know the 12 Rules for living a Fantastic Life. I always tell the people I coach that if you can practice even just one rule, or two or three to start, you'll be on your way to living the life you want. Eventually, as you master the first few Rules and make them a part of your life, the other Rules will dovetail with them. As you have learned in this book, the Rules are very much connected, and each one has its place in the grand scheme.

But none of these Rules will drive the results you want unless you do one last thing. You must be consistent with each of them. Consistency is the magic bullet everyone looks for, but few want to admit is absolutely critical to any success. Do you really have to work out almost every day from now until... forever, consistently, to get in shape and stay that way? Yes, you do.

When it comes to achieving anything in life, there is no shortage of desire. Everyone wants to make a lot of money, lose weight, get in shape, have a better marriage, establish a closer relationship with their children, find more spirituality, and so on. Those are big rock goals. The daily actions we like to take quickly as we dive in to achieve our goal is the sand.

Consistency happens when you do the GRAVEL work. It's that messy stuff in the middle that, when done right, makes traversing the daily sand all that much easier. And when something is easier, you'll do it more consistently.

How Long is a Long Time?

I've heard a few recent college grads who are now in the workforce complain that they worked really hard on a project. "I mean, we were working really hard for like, ninety days, and we didn't even get a bigger bonus," much to their dismay. What I'm saying with this last important chapter on Consistency is that in this world and in life, the biggest rewards do not come from sudden bursts of effort and then no effort or little effort after that. **The biggest rewards in life come from sustained high levels of effort. That's just the law of the universe.** So, to expect something monumental to come from a ninety-day effort is unrealistic. Life just doesn't work that way.

A long time is just that: a long time. It may be years and often decades before you realize the fully ripened fruits of sustained high-level effort. That cannot discourage you; let it excite you. The people you met in this book were selected because they have literally lived a lifetime delivering consistent effort toward their own Fantastic Lives. They followed one or more of the Rules in this book without a break for decades. There are patterns for success in life. This is one of them. They have persevered so consistently that the 12 Rules in this book are just part of who they are. If you're thinking, *"Thirty years* of busting my ass? Are you kidding me? That's not worth it." Then I say to you, "You have the wrong goals. You're seeking the wrong Fantastic Life, or you just have not found the real purpose to achieve." Until you have a real purpose, the work will seem monumental, and the Rules restricting. But when you have the right goals and the right purpose, the Rules and the work are actually fun and rewarding in and of themselves. That's why I say **the Fantastic Life is not a destination but a lifestyle.**

Let me be clear and counter what you might hear in many business blogs and books: Purpose does not have to be changing the world. It can be, but it doesn't have to be. **Purpose is found inside your goal, your resumes, and your clarity.** That is where motivation is found, created, and inspired. If you don't have motivation or discipline or drive to Do Nothing in Moderation, then go back and find it inside this book and these Rules. It's right here.

If you are looking at a health and fitness goal and you are consistent with a proven program, you will see big results in three to six months. If you stop once you get fit and trim, you won't stay that way. Sorry, but that's the truth. You'll have to continue with the program for as long as you want to stay healthy. If you want to learn a foreign language, give it at least a year of daily lessons. Then if you want to stay sharp and continue to learn, make speaking the language part of your everyday life. Let's say

BENJAMIN FRANKLIN SAID:
"Energy and persistence conquer all things."

you want to rise to a C-suite position in your company; it may take decades to get there. That's decades of consistently proving your abilities and leadership, with no "cheat days" where you get to be a knucklehead.

Do Less, Better, and with Consistency

Even if you say, "Craig, I'm going to set my goals and start with just one or two Rules," I'm cool with that so long as you live by those Rules and do them every day. You'll be so excited by your results that you'll want to add to your success. I just know it.

Let's say you want to get a dog and have it become a really great companion. A dog that is well mannered and good with everyone. Excellent goal! Well, there's only one way to do that. It's by dedicating time, attention, love, and training for hours and hours every single day. Consistently for the first two years, but really for the life of the dog. That means consistency of affection, consistency with praise, with commands, with reprimands, and using the same words, gestures, and rewards. When you do that, you will raise a dog that understands you and your desires. And you'll understand your dog's personality and desires. Like everything else in life, consistency is the key to success.

Consistency Builds Momentum

The best part about being consistent is that although the Rules might be hard at first, they get easier as you get going. I'm not saying they ever get easy. They don't. They get "easy-er." But you will continue to grow, to push yourself, and make your Fantastic Life fuller. Sometimes the hardest part of a Fantastic Life is getting out of bed. Once you're up and in the midst of your morning routine, it feels good. You feel alive, and continuing to the next part of your day is actually pretty awesome. The fact is, the more you do something, the better you get at it, the more used to it you become, and you hit your stride. It's like the runner's high. Those first few steps in a run, no matter who you are, might seem kind of sluggish, but within a few minutes and certainly within a few miles, it feels amazing. You get to ride the momentum of your effort.

If you haven't yet subscribed to my LIFEies, then now might be a good time to check out this weekly email where I take an article I find useful, boil it down to the most essential points, relate it to one of my 12 Fantastic Life Rules, and show you how to use it best. It's free, and I do these consistently, never missing a week—for a decade. LIFEies have amassed an audience tens of thousands strong as of this writing. They are engaged people who, like you, want to live a Fantastic Life.

Sign up for LIFEies at theFantasticLife.com

It may be years and often decades before you realize the fully ripened fruits of sustained high-level effort. That cannot discourage you; let it excite you.

The point here is that lots of people in the world have meaningful things to say. They start blogs, they begin doing podcasts, and get discouraged when only a few people read or tune in. It's the few who take the time to do the work of getting those words out and do it consistently enough to earn an audience. They quit and wonder why they aren't successful. I'm successful with LIFEies because I am consistent with LIFEies. I didn't start with a big following; it took consistent work and never giving up. Why? Because LIFEies keep me sharp and motivated. They are also my way of sharing the wisdom of others and showing how it fits into The Fantastic Life. It's as much for me as it is for you.

Consistency gets you on a roll. You don't waste time looking back to see where you left off. That's a huge time waster. Instead, you just pick up and run. That's momentum, and it breeds excitement and an energy all its own. Have you ever heard someone talk about a deal that dragged on and went south? Maybe it was a real estate deal, a business sale, or a merger. Maybe you've heard them say, "Time kills all deals." It's true. More deals die because they slow down in the process. One or both parties procrastinates, or stall and the deal falls apart. Consistently moving the deal forward a little bit or a lot every day is what gets it done.

A Fantastic Life is Yours to Live

Your Fantastic Life is waiting for you to get busy. To set your sights on what you want and use the Rules to live it with everything you do. Remember, the Fantastic Life is not a destination, it's a lifestyle choice that will set you up to have anything you want. So, first, you must choose and then follow the Rules in this book consistently. When you do, you'll be surprised by what you can and will accomplish. Your Fantastic Life is worth it.

the FANTASTIC LIFE® revisited

About Craig

Craig is an overachiever and maybe a little obsessed. But what successful innovator isn't? His creation is The Fantastic Life, a way of living that can help everyone live the life they've always wanted. Craig has spent decades formulating, living, and refining the 12 Rules and has used them to achieve goal after goal in fitness, career, family, relationships, health, and many other important areas of his life. He believes if he could do it, anyone can.

Craig was not born wealthy. He was not born of privilege. He grew up in a small Arizona town with five brothers and sisters. Throughout his years, Craig fostered a solid belief that once he decided to do something, doing it halfway was just a waste of time. So no matter what he did, he went for it.

This philosophy and his grand experiment of practicing the rules of The Fantastic Life have taken him around the world for business, sports, and adventure. He's scaled mountain peaks literally and figuratively. He's competed in the world's most grueling ultra-marathon endurance events, in the world's most challenging climates. He's made it to the top of his game, then changed the game and made it to the top of that one too. How? By, as Craig says, "Doing nothing in moderation."

the **FANTASTIC** LIFE revisited

Thank you for reading
The Fantastic Life.
If you enjoyed reading my book
please share your opinion with
others on Amazon.com.
I would love to hear what
you have to say and greatly
appreciate your support.

thefantasticlife.com

Made in the USA
Las Vegas, NV
08 January 2024